The Making of a C.R.I.S.I.S. Leader

The Making of a C.R.I.S.I.S. Leader

Sattar Bawany

BEP

BUSINESS EXPERT PRESS

Leader in applied, concise business books

First published in 2025 by
Business Expert Press, LLC
222 East 46th Street, New York, NY 10017
www.businessexpertpress.com

ISBN-13: 978-1-63742-784-2 (paperback)
ISBN-13: 978-1-63742-785-9 (e-book)

Business Expert Press Human Resource Management and Organizational Behavior Collection

First edition: 2025

10 9 8 7 6 5 4 3 2 1

Dedication

To my dearest Aisha,

You have been my anchor, my inspiration, and my greatest source of strength.
Your love, patience, and unwavering belief in me have made every milestone
possible. Through every challenge, your quiet wisdom and boundless support
have taught me the true meaning of partnership.

I dedicate it to you, not only as my wife but as my lifelong companion and
the heart of our shared journey.

With all my love and deepest gratitude, always and forever.

Description

The right leadership is critical for organizations to navigate successfully toward resolving insurmountable challenges in any crisis event. The book aims to help leaders at all levels unlearn and relearn effective crisis leadership.

Topics include the following:

- Lessons from past decades on how leaders respond successfully to crises.
- The best practice "C.R.I.S.I.S." leadership model that outlines the critical skills and competencies for leaders.
- How organizations can be better prepared for future crises.
- The board's role in navigating through organizational crises.

Contents

Testimonials

"The Making of a C.R.I.S.I.S. Leader provides a clear and practical guide for leading through uncertainty and disruption. With a focus on crisis management, Prof Bawany offers strategies for leaders to navigate and transform their organizations in the face of major challenges, regardless of the circumstances.

Prof Bawany emphasizes resilience, adaptability, and proactive planning, making this book essential for leaders at all levels. Through real-world examples and actionable insights, this book will equip readers with the skills to turn crises into opportunities for growth and transformation. This is a must-read for anyone leading in today's unpredictable environment."
—**Dr. Marshall Goldsmith is the Thinkers50 #1 Executive Coach and New York Times bestselling author of *The Earned Life, Triggers*, and *What Got You Here Won't Get You There*.**

"The Making of a C.R.I.S.I.S. Leader is a timely, well-researched, and comprehensive examination of leadership when it matters the most. Written with the sense of urgency that the context demands, Prof Bawany offers a memorable model, practical advice, and relevant case studies to guide leaders at all levels. This book should not just be read; it should be used to guide you when serious problems such as crises require immediate action."—**Jim Kouzes, Co-author of the bestselling *The Leadership Challenge* and a Fellow of the Doerr Institute for New Leaders, Rice University**

"The Making of a C.R.I.S.I.S. Leader is a how-to guide for leaders at all levels as they navigate the challenges in today's complex ever-changing world. The book provides practical tools for leaders during times of crisis and demonstrates the need to develop c-suite muscle memory to be ready to respond quickly and effectively when a crisis arises. The book is also like having your professional executive coach at your side. A must-read for all executives!"
—**The Honorable Chip Fulghum, Retired Col USAF and Former CFO and Deputy Undersecretary of Management at the Department of Homeland Security (DHS), Current CEO of Endeavors**

"One of the major challenges faced by contemporary organizations is to safeguard them in the event of a crisis. Crises originate in both the macroeconomic and global conditions on which the enterprise has no direct effect and which, when they arise, affect the business of the enterprise.

A crisis can thus disturb the balance of an enterprise. Fortunately, there are best practices tools, competencies to be adopted, and perspectives that leaders can use to steer their organizations during these difficult times, and these are found in the C.R.I.S.I.S. Leadership Model as expounded in Prof Sattar Bawany's latest book. The model provides businesses with the strategies to navigate unprecedented challenges while operating in a global environment that is increasingly volatile, uncertain, complex, ambiguous, and disruptive (VUCAD). A must-read for leaders across diverse organizations."
—**Pascal Bonet, Board Member, IAC —Intelligent Automation Advisory, Award-winning expert in AI and Automation, and author of the best-seller books** *Intelligent Automation* **and** *Irreplaceable.*

"Crisis management and leadership are more relevant and essential today than they ever have been. It is an understatement to say that the disruption we see today is more impactful and profound than what we have experienced in the past. It is at times like these that clarity of mind, confidence, and decisiveness is required. Prof Bawany provides exactly that in this book – breaking down complex puzzles into a smaller solvable challenge and laying out the roadmap for how leaders can tackle these challenges. The tools suggested are practical, relevant, and effective – coming from years of real-life experience and application.

The Making of a C.R.I.S.I.S. Leader *– an essential read for Crisis Management."*—**Ban-Seng Teh, Executive Vice President and Chief Commercial Officer Seagate Technology LLC, CA**

"In a crisis, communication in an organization isn't just a tool. It's the main factor that builds trust, fosters clarity, and inspires action. Leadership in a crisis is about speaking with transparency, listening with empathy, and guiding with clarity. The strongest leaders guide their teams through crises not with perfect answers but with authentic communication. Authentic communication is not about being perfect but it's about being real.

Prof. Sattar Bawany's latest book, The Making of a C.R.I.S.I.S. Leader, *is an essential read for leaders navigating corporate crises—those unexpected events that threaten an organization's reputation, financial stability, or operational continuity. This insightful book sheds light on the critical role of boards in every aspect of crisis management, particularly in ensuring that management decisions align with the long-term success and sustainability of the organization. A must-read for leaders and board members seeking to elevate their crisis management strategies."*—**Dato' Hj Che Abdullah Bin Mat Nawi, JP, Former Deputy Minister of Agriculture and Food Industry, Malaysia; former Kelantan State Councillor and CEO, UMK Holdings Sdn. Bhd.**

"I finished Prof Bawany's The Making of a C.R.I.S.I.S. Leader *on a flight to Europe and left the plane feeling both uncomfortable and assured. Prof Bawany succinctly raised the serious challenges posed by future crises facing all of us and outlined powerful frameworks to address them. I would recommend this book to those struggling to make sense of an increasingly complex world and how we can navigate it successfully."*—**Alizakri Alias, Board member, Petronas Dagangan and PruBSN Takaful and Trustee of Yayasan Hasanah and Yayasan Mahkota**

"In today's volatile and complex world, effective crisis leadership is more crucial than ever. Prof Sattar's book provides practical tools and insights for leaders to navigate disruptions with resilience and foresight. At QBE Singapore, we recognize that the ability to adapt, communicate effectively, and make agile decisions is key to thriving amid uncertainty. The C.R.I.S.I.S. Leadership Model and frameworks like these equip leaders to not only manage crises but to emerge stronger and more strategically focused. This book is an invaluable resource for anyone seeking to lead through the challenges of a rapidly changing landscape."—**Ronak Shah, CEO, QBE Insurance (Singapore)**

"Prof Sattar Bawany's book The Making of a C.R.I.S.I.S. Leader *is a readable and comprehensive guide that can benefit both senior management as well as aspiring business leaders. In my career, I've noticed that we usually plan for success but rarely for crises. However, recent experience has shown us that black swan events are now becoming more frequent, so this book is a*

timely reminder that good leadership should encompass planning for uncertainty."—**Richard Eu, Group Chairman, Eu Yan Sang International Ltd (EYSI)**

"*Prof. Sattar Bawany's latest book* The Making of a C.R.I.S.I.S. Leader *provides a comprehensive guide to the board and management in navigating through turbulent and challenging times.*"—**Datuk Syed Mohamed Ibrahim, President and CEO, Johor Corporation, Malaysia and Director, Sultan Ibrahim Foundation**

"*Having spent about 40 years as CEO and Managing Director of multinational companies and senior leadership in Singapore's public sector, I have experienced numerous unprecedented crises including the SARS and COVID that disrupted the world. Disruption is about finding innovative ways to stay relevant. I have learned that you cannot plan for it – but you need to learn to manage it when it comes. Prof Sattar's C.R.I.S.I.S. Leadership Model offers a practical crisis response framework that prepares a leader to build crisis resiliency in an organization. The book is a must-read for all business leaders in today's VUCAD-driven business environment.*"—**Ted Tan, Chairman, CSE Global Ltd and Former Deputy Chief Executive, Enterprise Singapore**

"*While day-to-day management is the responsibility of the executive team, the board must provide support while also critically evaluating management's actions to ensure they are effective and aligned with stakeholder interests.*

The Making of a C.R.I.S.I.S. Leader *is a best practice resource for directors to make tough decisions management that is critical during crises. It also provides guidance to the board in executing its role as a stabilizing force, providing strategic oversight, holding management accountable, ensuring transparency, and protecting the organization's value and reputation. A must-read for 21st century board directors.*"—**Rajeev Peshawaria, CEO, Stewardship Asia Center, Singapore, and President, Leadership Energy Consulting, Seattle, WA, USA. Author of the** *Wall Street Journal* **and Amazon bestseller** *Open-Source Leadership* **(McGraw Hill),** *Too Many Bosses, Too Few Leaders* **(Simon & Schuster)**

"*The Results-Based Leadership (RBL) Framework as expounded in* The Making of a C.R.I.S.I.S. Leader *is a powerful model that can guide boards in managing crises effectively by focusing on outcomes, aligning actions, and ensuring accountability. This approach prioritizes strategic impact over reactive responses, making it an essential tool for navigating organizational crises. The book provides board best practice approaches and guidelines for articulating a clear vision of success for the crisis response including setting a goal to maintain stakeholder trust, minimize operational disruptions, or safeguard the organization's reputation. By utilizing the RBL Framework, boards can move beyond reactive firefighting to a structured, outcome-focused approach that aligns immediate actions with long-term organizational resilience and success. A must-read for all CEOs and Board members*"—**Dato' Azmi Mohd Ali, Executive Chairman and Senior Partner, Azmi & Associates and Lifetime Fellow, Institute of Corporate Directors Malaysia (ICDM)**

"The Making of a C.R.I.S.I.S. Leader *delivers powerful insights and proven frameworks to empower today's leaders who facing a constant stream of unprecedented crises, uncertainty, and disruptive technological shifts with strategic agility, resilience, and confidence. It's a guide for leaders not just to adapt, but to lead their organizations forward with unshakable purpose and values.*"
—**Wianto Chen, President Director, MSIG Life Indonesia**

"*In an era marked by unprecedented global challenges—from geopolitical tensions to climate crises to the rapid disruption caused by technological innovation—leadership has never been more crucial. This book offers a timely and comprehensive guide for leaders at all levels, providing actionable insights and proven strategies to navigate through chaos and uncertainty. Prof Sattar Bawany's C.R.I.S.I.S. Leadership Model is particularly valuable, offering a structured approach to developing the critical skills and mindset necessary for managing crises effectively. By blending real-world case studies with forward-thinking frameworks, this book empowers leaders not only to survive in turbulent times but also to lead with resilience, agility, and purpose. A must-read for anyone looking to turn crises into opportunities for organizational growth and long-term success.*"—**Suhaimi Salleh, President and Group CEO, SSA Group**

"It is not just a VUCA world, but a VUCAD world, one that is not only volatile, uncertain, complex, and ambiguous but also disruptive. Organizations will need to prepare for the disruptive challenges that will come their way, and Leadership is key.

The C.R.I.S.I.S. leadership model provides a useful frame for leaders, especially in leading an organization during times of crisis. Prof Sattar Bawany also provides useful guides for both the Board and Management, to take the necessary steps to hone their skills, so that they can protect the organization when a crisis occurs."—**Sim Gim Guan, Executive Director, Singapore National Employers Federation (SNEF)**

"In the crowded field of books about leadership, Prof Sattar Bawany's book The Making of a C.R.I.S.I.S Leader *truly stands out. It situates the challenge of leadership in our era squarely in the context of ongoing crises and disruption, where non-linear change suddenly manifests itself. Prof Bawany lays out the disciplines needed when executing leadership tasks in such an environment. For example, a crisis impacts team dynamics and calls for a changed leadership style toward great decision-making decentralization. To my mind, the key discipline he describes is to see crises as an opportunity for organizational transformation and the acquisition of competitive advantages, rather than retreating into survival mode and seeing the crisis merely as a storm to be weathered.*

Through concrete case examples, Prof Bawany outlines how leaders in crisis conditions need to dive deep within their organizations and within themselves to turn crisis into opportunity. Through his explanation of the C.R.I.S.I.S. model of leadership, he also touches on various best practices, such as the need for transparent and empathetic communications in a crisis – something the Soviets and the Japanese military during the Second World War spectacularly failed to do, with predictable results. Prof Bawany eloquently makes the case for why, in our era, organizations should not be built for stability but built for change, with argues for prioritizing the attributes of agility and, above all, resilience."—**Leon Perera, Chairman of the Board, Yamada Consulting and Spire; Board Director, Humanitarian Organization for Migration Economics and Former Member of Parliament in Singapore**

"It feels undoubtedly true that leaders of today will need to deal with greater complexity which will come at speed and unpredictability. Climate change alone will require leaders of government, business, and civil society to have remarkable leadership capacities to navigate this future world. This is just one of many significant phenomena, we are now facing. Prof Sattar's new book, The Making of a C.R.I.S.I.S. Leader, *presents thought-provoking and immediately useful tools and notions to equip every leader to take on these challenges and become a stronger force for good. These tools include how to prepare for a crisis, how to coach leaders to be ready for this new world, and how boards should provide oversight of their organizations in this new context."*—**Simon (Mac) McKenzie, CEO, the Bridge Institute**

"In The Making of a C.R.I.S.I.S. Leader, *Professor Sattar Bawany offers an insightful and comprehensive guide for leaders navigating the complex, volatile, and interconnected landscape of today's global crises. Drawing on a wide range of real-world examples, from geopolitical conflicts to corporate disasters, this book highlights the urgent need for effective crisis management strategies in an era marked by uncertainty and disruption. Professor Bawany not only examines past crises but also equips leaders with the tools and frameworks necessary to lead organizations through future challenges. His innovative C.R.I.S.I.S. Leadership Model offers a practical approach to developing the critical skills and competencies needed to thrive under pressure. A must-read for anyone in a leadership position, this book is a vital resource for learning how to transform moments of crisis into opportunities for growth, resilience, and long-term sustainability. Whether you're leading a corporation, a community, or a country, Professor Bawany's expertise will inspire you to lead with clarity and confidence in the face of adversity."*—**Prof. Dr. Vinitha Guptan, Vice-Chancellor, Saito University College**

"Having been in multiple global roles around the world, I have had my share of dealing with crises affecting thousands of employees and external stakeholders and fully relate to Prof Bawany's book and its great insights on dealing with crises beyond a leader's control. His real-life examples and conceptual models will help leaders at all levels to demonstrate individual and organizational resilience to reshape the outcomes of the future.

The need to envision a purpose-driven future to reinvent the organization is fully aligned with what we do for employees and leaders on personal Purpose, Energy, and Values, for them to remain relevant. Highly recommend this timely book, as the world goes through one crisis after another and needs leaders with the ability, capacity, and resilience to deal with it."—**Varun Bhatia, CEO eVolv and Ex CHRO of Levi Strauss, AirAsia, and Global HR leader at Gillette, P&G, and Kraft Foods**

"The latest Professor Sattar Bawany's book will guide the organization to adopt proactive strategies to tackle future crises, leveraging leadership skills and frameworks to navigate an increasingly disruptive world. Effective leadership is crucial for resolving crises, with the book aiming to teach leaders at all levels the C.R.I.S.I.S. Leadership Model.

This book is a must-read for all leaders to guide them in navigating the uncertainties of the business world. It offers a comprehensive toolkit for crisis management, empowering leaders with the knowledge and skills needed to effectively steer their organizations through turbulent times. By adopting the strategies outlined in this book, leaders can enhance their decision-making capabilities, foster resilience, and ensure long-term sustainability amidst an ever-changing landscape."—**Amran Zakaria, Head, Group Human Capital Division, Johor Plantations Group Berhad**

"As an educator, I can wholeheartedly testify that teachers are constantly operating on the principles of C.R.I.S.I.S. outlined in this book. Imagine managing a classroom of 30 students—it's crisis management daily. Throughout history, good teachers have naturally employed many of the powerful principles advocated here, such as communication (where active listening is essential for successful teaching and learning), risk management (anticipating challenges with students or the classroom environment), influence (motivating and guiding students toward learning), strategizing (planning lessons and handling unexpected situations), inspiring (keeping students engaged and motivated), and sustaining (ensuring a productive learning environment amidst disruptions). I resonate with these principles not only in the classroom but also in the broader context of corporate leadership. Whether in education or business, transformational leadership requires the same skills and competencies highlighted in this highly relevant and practical book."—**Ky. Col. Prof.**

Dr. Edward Roy Krishnan, Founder and Director General, European International University (EIU-Paris)

"Professor Satar Bawany's The Making of a C.R.I.S.I.S Leader *is more than a manual for navigating tough times—it's a roadmap for transforming challenges into leadership opportunities. In an era where change is swift, and crises feel almost constant, this book dives deeply into the qualities leaders need to rise above adversity, steering their teams and organizations toward sustainable success. Prof Bawany's unique C.R.I.S.I.S. framework resonates with authenticity and practicality, blending his extensive experience with actionable insights. For leaders new to their roles, this book provides foundational skills to navigate high-pressure situations with clarity and purpose. Having spent years in leadership myself, I've learned that true resilience is not about weathering one storm but knowing how to rise, adapt, and inspire through every wave. Professor Bawany's book encapsulates this ethos perfectly. I wholeheartedly endorse this book as a must-read for today's and tomorrow's leaders."*—**Datuk Jake Abdullah, Consultant Media Prima Audio, CEO Malaysian Dynamic Media**

The Making of a C.R.I.S.I.S. Leader *is an essential playbook for navigating through uncertainty and disruption. Prof Sattar Bawany distills the essence of crisis leadership, offering a structured C.R.I.S.I.S. model that leaders can apply to respond effectively when the stakes are high. His insights go beyond mere crisis management—they empower leaders to turn challenges into opportunities for resilience and growth.*

The book's approach to communication, resilience, and strategic intelligence equips leaders with the mental and emotional tools necessary for navigating complex environments. It also underscores the importance of preparation, including proactive crisis planning and coaching at the board level, to ensure that when disruption strikes, leaders are ready to respond with clarity and confidence. This book is not just for executives; it's a comprehensive guide for anyone seeking to enhance their leadership capabilities in today's unpredictable world. It provides actionable frameworks and real-world examples, helping leaders stay adaptable and prepared to transform a crisis into a catalyst for positive change. Prof Bawany's work is essential reading for anyone committed to leading effectively through turbulent times."—**Terry O'Connor OBE, Managing Director, Trim Consultancy and former CEO, PT Matahari Department Store Tbk, Indonesia and former Managing Director and CEO, Courts Asia**

"*Boards should routinely assess organizational resilience and identify potential vulnerabilities. This involves scenario planning, stress testing, and simulations to pre-emptively understand the impact of various crises (e.g., financial, operational, reputational).* The Making of a C.R.I.S.I.S. Leader *provides best practices and research-based leadership tools and frameworks that guide boards in managing crises by equipping board members with structured approaches and principles for rapid, yet prudent, decision-making. Below is a framework that addresses key components for effective board leadership in crises.*

The book offers a comprehensive guide for boards to navigate crises with foresight, agility, and accountability, ensuring they protect organizational integrity while being responsive to stakeholders. I would highly recommend it to all Board members from various industries globally."—**Tan Sri Dato' Azman Shah Haron, Chairman and CEO, Holiday Villa Hotels and Resorts Limited, former President of the Malaysia Employers Federation (MEF), and former President of the International Organization of Employers (IOE)**

"*Prof. Sattar Bawany's latest book* The Making of a C.R.I.S.I.S. Leader *provides the board of directors with best practice approaches and guidance on how they could play a pivotal role in managing organizational crises, as they are responsible for overseeing the company's long-term stability and safeguarding stakeholders' interests. When a crisis emerges—be it financial, reputational, operational, or strategic—the board's actions are instrumental in navigating the organization through turbulent times. The board is responsible for ensuring that the organization has a crisis management plan and is prepared to handle emergencies. The book guides the board during times of crisis on how they could navigate the organization's strategic direction and approves major decisions that affect the company's long-term viability. A must-read for members of boards for all types of organizations.*"—**Edy Tuhirman, Founder, Kaya Investing Platform and former President Director and CEO of Generali Indonesia**

"Definitely The Making of a CR.I.S.I.S. Leader *is a book not to be missed. Prof. Sattar Bawany expertly distils the many messages and learnings from headwinds faced by leaders in recent years, captured in this book. And in a world that is transitioning, you will want to read this book and continue to go back to it as you take on the more to come."*—**Datuk (Dr) Nora Manaf, Group Chief Human Capital Officer, Maybank and Board Member, Etiqa General Insurance Berhad, MBB Labs (Bangalore), India**

"In a world marked by continuous disruption and unforeseen challenges, Prof Sattar Bawany's The Making of a C.R.I.S.I.S. Leader *emerges as a vital resource for today's leaders. This book encapsulates the essence of adaptive and resilient leadership, equipping readers with the insights and tools to manage crises with foresight and confidence. Prof Bawany's unique C.R.I.S.I.S. Leadership Model is a comprehensive guide that goes beyond mere survival, emphasizing transformation and strategic agility.*

Drawing from real-world examples and practical wisdom, this work offers an indispensable roadmap for executives and managers striving to lead in volatile, uncertain, complex, and ambiguous environments. Prof Bawany's approach is both enlightening and empowering, making this book a must-read for anyone committed to navigating the complexities of modern leadership."—**Adj. Prof Farid Basir, Group Chief People Officer, MBSB and Adjunct Professor, UNITAR International University, Kuala Lumpur, Malaysia**

"Prof. Sattar Bawany's The Making of a C.R.I.S.I.S. Leader *presents a compelling and practical approach to crisis management with the 'C.R.I.S.I.S.' model, a framework deeply rooted in research and designed for modern-day leadership. Each component—Communication, Resilience, Intelligence, Shifting the Mental Model, Inspiring, and Setting the Recovery Path—is a meticulously crafted tool, empowering leaders to steer their teams with empathy, resilience, and foresight. Bawany's insights on maintaining transparency, fostering trust, and implementing data-driven decision-making during disruptions make this book an invaluable resource for leaders who aspire to not only manage crises but inspire and transform their organizations through them."*—**Dr. Timothy Low, Former CEO of Gleneagles Hospital and former CEO and Board Director of Farrer Park Hospital**

"In The Making of a C.R.I.S.I.S. Leader, *Prof Sattar Bawany offers an insightful and indispensable guide for leaders navigating the turbulent waters of today's volatile, uncertain, complex, ambiguous, and disruptive global environment. This book is a masterclass in crisis leadership that fuses theoretical insights with actionable strategies and real-world case studies. Aspiring and seasoned leaders alike will find Prof Bawany's 5-step crisis management planning and strategy an invaluable resource to steer their organizations through crises and emerge stronger. His focus on transparent communication, stakeholder engagement, strategic agility, and a culture of continuous learning is both timely and timeless.*

I thank Prof Bawany for sharing his wisdom and thoughts on becoming a more effective, agile and resilient leader."—**Dr. Kelvin Koh W B, Medical Director, Jurong Community Hospital and Adjunct Assistant Professor, Department of Medicine, NUS Yong Loo Lin School of Medicine, National University of Singapore**

"Disruption is all around us, more so today than ever before. And given the trajectory that the world is taking over the coming decades, this area of disruption is going to be even more emphatic than ever. The impact of this on the vision of the Board, on the strategies of the CEO and the Management Team, as well as how work is being done to achieve those strategic goals now has led to the rise of a very different leader, a C.R.I.S.I.S Leader. In this book by Prof Sattar, he goes on to explore what it takes to be an effective leader in disruptive times, but he also goes on to provide a variety of pragmatic frameworks that can be practically applied to overcome the challenges many leaders face today. The Paragon7 Cognitive Readiness Competencies Framework, as well as Results Based Leadership Framework, are 2 such tools that can be applied with relative ease by the leaders of organizations.

As a Board Member myself, the questions raised by Prof Sattar certainly resonate with me and I believe they should take front and center stage at all yearly board evaluation exercises. A definite must-have on the reading list of board members and senior management team members as well as those aspiring to reach the upper echelons of management as part of their career development."—**Taranjeet Singh, CEO, Quantum Steppe Advisory and**

Advisory Panel Member for Universiti Teknologi Petronas, Malaysia, and Trustee Board Member, Esil University, Astana, Kazakhstan

"*The Making of a* C.R.I.S.I.S. *Leader by Professor Sattar Bawany offers a timely and indispensable roadmap for leaders navigating an era of extraordinary disruption and uncertainty. In this powerful work, Professor Bawany synthesizes insights from interviews with C-suite leaders worldwide, unveiling the essential practices that help leaders not only survive but thrive in crises. His 'C.R.I.S.I.S.' model breaks down critical dimensions of leadership during crisis events: Communicating effectively and empathetically, building Resilience to manage stress, ensuring Intelligence with data-driven insights, fostering Strategic agility, and inspiring Support among teams.*

With compelling case studies — including the global responses to the COVID-19 pandemic — Professor Bawany showcases real-world applications of his framework, highlighting how leaders can develop adaptability, communicate transparently, and transform crises into opportunities for growth. This book is a comprehensive guide to mastering the art of crisis leadership and an essential resource for any leader committed to resilience, agility, and the sustained success of their organization in uncertain times."—**Dr. Tan Joo Seng, Associate Professor, Nanyang Business School, Nanyang Technological University, Singapore**

"*The book provides practical and useful tools and approaches to help leaders hone the right competencies and adopt balanced perspectives on crisis management. In the world of VUCA where transformative leadership needs to occur, the C.R.I.S.I.S. Leadership Model provides a systematic overarching approach to navigating the myriads of challenges that many leaders face. I am confident the reader will find this book extremely useful and enlightening. I recommend this book to all organizational leaders, new or experienced.*"—**Dr. Tham Tat Yean, Chief Executive Officer, Frontier Healthcare Group and Ag Country Head, Qualitas Health, Singapore**

"*In the last 100 years the world faced a series of crises—starting with the great depression of 1929, the wars, the oil crisis, the financial crises of Asia and the world and then the COVID-19 pandemic. Many lessons have been learned from these. How do we deal with future crises, which the world will no doubt face? With useful case studies, Sattar gives an insight into how leaders can prepare for the next crisis and beyond."*—**Prof Inderjit Singh Dhaliwal, President of the Global Startup Committee, World Business Angles Investment Forum (WBAF), Adjunct Professor, Nanyang Technological University, Singapore**

"Crisis management and leadership are two important and often time intertwining skillsets, that are often learned through experience with trials, tribulations, and perhaps errors in one's career & life. Professor Bawany's insights on crisis leadership are exemplary offering a practical guide with pearls of wisdom in helping anyone to navigate through these uncharted territories. Kudos to Prof Bawany for excellent work!"—**Joe Tai, Regional Chief Operating Officer and Managing Director, APAC, TP Aerospace**

"Professor Bawany's latest work is relevant to senior leaders and their management teams, as they navigate through very unsettling times. In recent times, the pace of technological change has accelerated with the advent of AI, geopolitical tension has increased in Eastern Europe and the Middle East, and several key developed economies have seen significant changes in leadership and international policy. The landscape for large multinational companies has never been so complex and unpredictable. Professor Bawany can link real-world events to the behaviors of leaders and the decisions they take in response to the risks and opportunities they face each day. This book is a valuable resource for senior leaders who are seeking an edge in understanding what drives high-performing individuals and teams, and how they can be better leaders in times of crisis."—**Simon Sinclair, COO, Markets Trading, Standard Chartered Bank**

"In the dynamic and often tumultuous realm of business, few books carve out a distinct and indispensable niche as seamlessly as Prof Sattar Bawany's new book, The Making of a C.R.I.S.I.S. Leader. *"It's a rigorous exploration and insightful examination of the qualities that define and distinguish truly transformative leaders in times of crisis. Through compelling case studies and robust research, Bawany offers a lucid framework for understanding the*

complexities of leadership when the stakes are highest. His 'C.R.I.S.I.S.' model of leadership—Communicate, Resilience, Intelligence, Shifting the Mental Model—does more than iterate; it inspires."—**Robin Speculand, Author of** ***Implement and World's Best Bank***

"As a CEO who has faced numerous crises, it's become evident that crises are happening more frequently and with greater intensity. In these moments, stakeholders—employees, clients, and partners—look to their leaders for stability and direction more than ever before. Sattar Bawany's The Making of a C.R.I.S.I.S. Leader *arrives at a critical time, offering leaders a clear and practical framework for navigating these unpredictable challenges. The C.R.I.S.I.S. model emphasizes the importance of communication, resilience, and strategic agility, all of which are indispensable for today's leaders."* —**Brian O. Underhill, Ph.D., PCC, Founder and CEO, Coach Source, LLC**

"Professor Sattar's take on the role of the Board when handling a crisis is both comprehensive and practical. He offers many considerations and useful tips on what Boards need to do, before, during, and after a crisis. In the current business climate where multiple complexities exist on many fronts, it makes great sense for Boards and Leadership to work closely hand in hand to anticipate and proactively respond to crises and emerge stronger to benefit the organizations."—**Carmen Wee, MA, IHRP-MP, SID SRAD, Board Member, HTX & Workforce Singapore**

"Disruption seems to be the new normal as the modern world oscillates between the opportunities afforded by radical technologies and the macro-risks of economic uncertainties or geopolitical conflict. Hence it is not unknown to see leaders today waking up to a new crisis with the same regularity as the morning alarm. This makes Prof Bawany's manifesto on Crisis Leadership a pertinent and well-timed reminder of the first principles that result in true leadership during turbulent times."—**Gyan Nagpal, Director of Human Resources—AIA Group/Dean of AIA Leadership Centre and author of the award-winning bestsellers** ***The Future Ready Organisation*** **(2020) and** ***Talent Economics*** **(2013)**

"Congrats to Prof Sattar for embarking on this endeavor to refresh and share ideas and best practices to lead in a disruptive, digitalized, and divisive global world order. This is useful reading to further guide and steer our future-ready leadership and thinking particularly in the globe impacted by the Generative Artificial Intelligence and Sustainability agenda."—**Patrick Tay Teck Guan, BBM, Assistant Secretary-General, National Trades Union Congress (NTUC) and Member of Parliament of Singapore, Pioneer Constituency**

"This book is a very timely addition to the existing scholarly and professional literature on managerial approaches to a crisis at both societal and organizational levels. Given the plethora of short-term and longer-term crises occurring across the world, whether man-made, environmental, or some combination of these, this book provides an extremely timely and reassuring guide for managers and leaders on how to effectively and strategically respond when their interests or desired outcomes are threatened. It combines a summary and critique of contemporary crisis management theory and practice with an innovative 'C.R.I.S.I.S.' (communication-resilience-intelligence-shifting mental model-inspiring-structuring the recovery plan) framework which will undoubtedly be welcomed by those charged with the management of diverse crises."—**Professor Alan Nankervis, Professor of Human Resource Management, Curtin University**

"The importance of Leadership in a crisis cannot be over-emphasized. You have beautifully captured the essence of leadership in such crises and provided an extremely useful 'C.R.I.S.I.S.' leadership framework and various case studies for Leaders to successfully manage disruptions in a crisis. Your emphasis on preparing for crisis and creating crisis management plans will create the foundations for companies to deal with disruptions effectively and hopefully, prevent them from developing into crises. Your point on the Board taking the lead in setting the tone and pace of crisis preparedness in a company is timely. In today's VUCAD environment, Boards need to take a proactive stance and where necessary, 'coach' and guide management accordingly. Your chapter on 'Coaching for C.R.I.S.I.S. Leaders' resonates with me as I have personally benefited from executive coaching, and I strongly recommend it for every Leader.

This book is a must-read for all Leaders preparing for the next crisis!"
—**BG (Retd) Chua Chwee Koh, Former Chief Operating Officer, Certis CISCO Pte Ltd and Board Director of Nasdaq-listed Trident Digital Tech Holdings Ltd and SGX-listed companies, Addvalue Technologies Ltd and Raffles Education Ltd**

"It is critical in today's world to be able to competently lead through a crisis and come out stronger. This book teaches you how to precisely do that. It is an excellent read!"—**Professor Jochen Wirtz, Vice Dean, MBA Programmes and Professor of Marketing, National University of Singapore**

"Prof Sattar Bawany's book The Making of a C.R.I.S.I.S. Leader *beautifully captures the essence of the theme of Crisis Leadership. It indeed positions itself as a valuable guide for anyone looking to enhance their leadership capabilities in an increasingly unpredictable world. Prof Bawany's holistic approach, addressing crises at personal, familial, institutional, corporate, and political levels, makes the book a versatile resource for individuals across various spheres.*

By acknowledging that every crisis carries growth potential, Prof Bawany empowers leaders and individuals to not just manage crises but to emerge stronger from them. His analysis of the complex dynamics of leadership during times of uncertainty provides readers with the tools needed to adapt, innovate, and thrive in the face of adversity as well as serves as a roadmap for navigating both professional and personal challenges during crises is spot on. Whether you're leading a company, or government institution, or dealing with societal or political disruptions, the lessons in The Making of a C.R.I.S.I.S. Leader *will equip you with strategies that foster resilience, agility, and long-term success."*—**Datuk Seri Mohamed Iqbal Rawther, Group Deputy Chairman of Farlim Group (Malaysia) Berhad; Pro-Chancellor, Binary University Malaysia and former Chairman of the Business Advisory Council, United Nations Economic and Social Commission for Asia and the Pacific**

"Prof Sattar elegantly summarises the key principle underpinning the C.R.I.S.I.S. leadership model, including the management plan and strategy and the underlying reasons. He communicates the lessons and learnings

in a simple, practical, easily internalized, and applicable manner through well-summarised text and comprehensive summary diagrams. An excellent reflective read for all categories of leaders up to the C suite level."—**Adjunct Associate Professor Bernard Thong, Chairman Medical Board, Tan Tock Seng Hospital and National Healthcare Group**

"*The Making of a C.R.I.S.I.S. Leader by Sattar Bawany is a compelling guide to navigating the complexities of leadership in turbulent times. Bawany outlines in well-researched detail how leaders can thrive by embracing uncertainty and fostering resilience. The book's C.R.I.S.I.S. leadership framework provides a clear, actionable roadmap for decision-making and emotional intelligence under pressure. This book urges readers to see crises as opportunities for growth and transformation. Packed with real-world insights and case studies, it is a timely and valuable resource. A must-read for leaders aiming to ensure their organizations will excel in the current challenging business and social environment.*"—**Ken Pasternak, Author, Speaker, Educator, Member of Marshall Goldsmith's 100 Coaches Community**

"*Your perspective is insightful—crisis and opportunity often coexist, and the pace at which technology, particularly internet communication, has accelerated change is unprecedented. The digital revolution is reshaping sectors like politics, economics, society, and technology, making the world more interconnected and, as you mentioned, commoditized.*

Leaders today face a complex landscape where the challenges and opportunities shift quickly, and this is where management models become critical. The book The Making of a CR.I.S.I.S. Leader *offers these models which are invaluable, as it could provide leaders with the tools to navigate these rapid changes and adapt to new norms, ensuring they can thrive in this era of transformation. Your framing captures the urgency and relevance of such guidance in a world where constant adaptation is necessary for success.*"—**YM Tengku Tan Sri (Dr) Mahaleel Tengku Arif, Former Group Chief Executive Officer of Proton Holdings Berhad, Former Director, Nestle Malaysia and Shell Malaysia**

"*In the context of ongoing global crises, such as wars, economic instability, climate change, social unrest, and health emergencies, Professor Sattar Bawany has written a timely book which clearly articulates the attributes corporate leaders must develop such as resilience, disruptive digital mindset, and cognitive readiness to mention a few, to guide their organizations through crises, ensuring not only survival but also the potential for growth and positive impact in the world."*—**Prof. Dr. Milé Terziovski, Chair, Department of Business Technology and Entrepreneurship (BTE), Professor of Entrepreneurship and Innovation, President, Swinburne University Staff Club, Swinburne University of Technology, Melbourne, Australia**

"Prof. Sattar's insightful latest book The Making of a C.R.I.S.I.S. Leader *is a must-read for leaders navigating the complexities of crisis management. His analysis not only highlights the critical need for unlearning outdated practices but also emphasizes the importance of relearning effective strategies to lead through turbulent times.*

Prof. Sattar's expertise and clear articulation make this review an invaluable resource for leaders at all levels seeking to enhance their crisis leadership skills. Highly recommended for anyone committed to driving positive change and resilience in their organizations."—**Anndy Lian, Intergovernmental Blockchain Expert and Best-selling Book Author**

*"*The Making of a C.R.I.S.I.S. Leader *by Prof. Bawany is a timely guide for leaders navigating an increasingly complex world. His C.R.I.S.I.S. Leadership Model provides an actionable framework for building the resilience and adaptability essential to leading during crises. This is more than a theoretical concept—it's a model grounded in the realities of modern leadership, offering practical tools that leaders can apply immediately.*

The book's focus on Crisis Management Planning is particularly valuable, with its structured five-step approach equipping leaders to prepare their organizations for the unexpected. Additionally, the insights on the board's role in crisis navigation offer crucial guidance for governance teams, underscoring the strategic importance of leadership at every level. For leaders committed to long-term organizational resilience, this book is an invaluable resource."
—**Ryan Lim, MSID, Founding Partner, QED Changemakers**

"A crisis can quickly expose a leader's hidden strengths and weaknesses. Many books are written about crisis management, but few focus on crisis leadership.

Managing and providing leadership in a crisis is not the same, although each addresses different aspects of a difficult situation. Don't wait until a crisis strikes to find out your leadership skills are wanting in these areas. The book The Making of a C.R.I.S.I.S. Leader *provides the best practice resource guide on the skills, competencies, traits, and perspectives a leader needs to demonstrate effectively in a crisis."*—**Bill Lang, Executive Director, Small Business Australia, Chairman, Bill Lang International, Executive Chairman, Human Performance Company**

"Prof Sattar has filled a gap in the market with The Making of a C.R.I.S.I.S. Leader *putting crisis management at the senior most leadership levels front and center. This is essential reading for all leaders, entrepreneurs, start-ups and scale-ups, as they continue to navigate increasingly unpredictable social, economic, and geo-political times, with ongoing business transformation continuing at a pace. A great read with practical frameworks and models for leaders to apply directly to their business, now."*—**Jeremy Blain, CEO Performance Works International. #1 internationally best-selling author of** *Unleash The Inner CEO – Make distributed leadership a reality*—**The 'Leadership Book of the Year' winner at the Global Book Awards, 2024**

"Good leadership is crucial in a crisis, providing the clarity, direction, and decisiveness needed to navigate uncertainty. A strong leader keeps the team focused, boosts morale, and makes tough decisions that mitigate risks and drive recovery. Effective crisis leadership also requires clear communication, empathy, and adaptability to manage both immediate challenges and long-term impacts. The publication, The Making of a C.R.I.S.I.S. Leader, *by Professor Sattar Bawany offers valuable lessons on crisis management, the skills leaders need to handle future disruptions and how they can transform organizations. It draws from the experiences of leaders, offering insights into decision-making, innovation, and building confidence in turbulent times."*—**Hernaikh Singh, Deputy Director, Institute of South Asian Studies (ISAS), National University of Singapore (NUS)**

"Business environment has become more hostile and unpredictable. Professor Bawany's 5-step crisis management planning and strategy provides some

brilliant insights into managing crises and prepares leaders to navigate uncertain futures. A timely and well-written book."—**Kenny Yap, Executive Chairman, Qian Hu Corporation Limited**

"I think the book The Making of a C.R.I.S.I.S. Leader *is an exceptional work that provides leaders with the tools and wisdom needed to steer the organizations through turbulent times. I especially like the best practice tool on the Paragon[7] cognitive readiness framework. Wish you all the best with your latest book!"*—**Shamsol Anuar Ibrahim, Head Group Human Capital, DRB-HICOM Berhad**

"I am amazed at the author's thoughts to emphasize new dimensions of leadership. The C.R.I.S.I.S Leadership model is very relevant and timely for the current and robust environment where organizations require resilient and agile leaders who believe in sustainability. The R.B.L. Framework and A.D.A.M. Coaching Model provide a great direction. Well done!" —**Dr. Roselina A. Saufi, Professor in Business and Management and former Dean, Malaysian Graduate School of Entrepreneurship and Business, University Malaysia Kelantan**

"As the saying goes 'The taste of the pudding is in the eating'. This book offers a timely, insightful, and practical guide for leaders navigating an increasingly VUCAD World. Professor Bawany's expertise shines through in his analysis of leadership during crises, providing not only theoretical frameworks but also real-world examples of leadership in action. The C.R.I.S.I.S. model he introduces is a comprehensive blueprint for leaders who seek to excel in moments of extreme uncertainty and challenge. This book is an essential read for any leader who aspires to lead in addressing the growing complexity of global crises, which are reshaping the business landscape and necessitating robust crisis management skills."—**Mohar Ibrahim, Founder MMI Associates and Former Senior Advisor, Group Human Resources, Sapura Energy Berhad**

"The Making of a C.R.I.S.I.S. Leader is a must-read for leaders at all levels navigating today's unpredictable world. Professor Bawany's actionable framework equips readers with the skills to turn crises into opportunities for growth and transformation. This book is a valuable resource for anyone seeking to

lead effectively in times of disruption."—**Virendra Shelar, Executive Officer and President, Omron Management Center Asia Pacific and General Manager, Global Human Resource Strategy Department**

"In crises, harnessing the strengths of a diverse team can lead to innovative solutions. A crisis leader should promote collaboration, encouraging insights from varied perspectives to navigate challenges more effectively. While crises often arise unexpectedly, a strong leader prepares for potential issues through scenario planning and risk assessment. Afterward, reflecting on what worked and what didn't cultivates a learning mindset, refining strategies, and enhancing future responses, which fosters a culture of continuous improvement. Prof. Sattar emphasizes that by showing empathy, actively listening, and supporting their team, leaders can sustain morale and trust during tough times. Resilience and viewing challenges as opportunities for growth are crucial.

I commend Prof Sattar for dedicating considerable time to this field of study, drawing on his management experience and interactions with CEOs and entrepreneurs, enabling him to grasp the nuances of the current business landscape."—**Dr. T. Chandroo, Chairman and CEO, MMI Group**

"Executive coaching for emerging leaders during a crisis requires unique strategies to foster resilience, adaptability, and strategic thinking. The A.D.A.M. Coaching Framework, as detailed in The Making of a C.R.I.S.I.S. Leader*, offers a structured model for executive coaches, providing a clear pathway toward goal achievement. This framework also includes an action phrase that empowers clients to embrace self-discovery and develop an action plan that instills accountability.*

This book is particularly timely, offering crucial guidance to executive coaches in times of crisis."—**Dr. Michael Heah, MCC, Chairman, Malaysian Association of Certified Coaches and CEO and Founder, Corporate Coach Academy Sdn Bhd**

"We are living in an era where both the scale and impact of disruption have never been greater. Prof Sattar's latest book on leading during such challenging times provides a timely response in the form of a robust conceptual framework, that is equally applicable for both individuals practicing self-mastery and for leaders of teams and organizations who are enabling their organization in

navigating through such unchartered territories. Just like a sextant in the hands of a capable navigator, the C.R.I.S.I.S. framework facilitates the mapping of strategy to mitigate against potential threats during such turbulent and chaotic times."—**John Augustine Ong, Learning & Development, Qatar Investment Authority**

"The Making of a C.R.I.S.I.S. Leader by Professor Sattar Bawany offers profound insights and essential practical tools for leaders navigating today's turbulent business environment. The integrated 'C.R.I.S.I.S.' approach redefines how organizations respond effectively to threats that could jeopardize their survival, making this work a critical guide for crisis leadership."
—**Dr. Amer Ali Al-Atwi, Professor of Organizational Behavior, University of Al-Qadisiyah , Iraq**

"In The Making of a C.R.I.S.I.S. Leader, readers will discover a comprehensive and timely guide for navigating the complexities of modern leadership. This book offers a valuable roadmap for leaders at all levels, providing practical strategies and tools to address the challenges of today's fast-paced and unpredictable world. The A.D.A.M. coaching methodology is a game-changer for developing leaders who can effectively manage crisis and uncertainty. The C.R.I.S.I.S. leadership model and crisis management strategies presented in this book are impactful, offering a clear and actionable framework for leaders to follow.

This book is a must-read for anyone looking to develop their leadership skills and stay ahead of the curve in today's disruptive global environment. The insights and expertise shared within these pages will empower leaders to navigate even the most turbulent of times confidently."—**Jesline Su (MHRM), Director, Human Resources & Corporate Services and Board Member, Lighthouse Evangelism**

CHAPTER 1

Leadership During Times of Crisis

As the business community has learned through the COVID-19 pandemic, it's more important than ever for leaders to anticipate and plan for the possibility of an unplanned disruptive or crisis event. The more prepared you are to manage shocks, the less likely you'll fall victim to the serious harm a crisis has the potential to inflict.

We face a new era of radical uncertainty and disruption brought about by other challenges such as climate change, financial crises, terrorism, demographic changes in the labor market, health/disease risk from the pandemic, and rapid developments in innovative digital technologies and their impact on workplace transformation.

Over the past 20 years, successive economic and geopolitical crises have quickly sent shockwaves throughout the world, affecting every country, economy, trading relationship, and business operation. Amid continuing uncertainty around how the war in Ukraine may end or escalate, business leaders face the challenges of navigating in the dark, accelerating already urgent transformation plans, and building organizational resilience for impacts that may yet strike.

The New Realities

The war on Ukraine. The COVID pandemic. Natural disasters. These occurrences raise alarms about the lack of readiness for what is to come and spark recognition that many major events, no matter their origin, tend to have ripple effects.

Take the current supply chain disruption faced by many countries— while only occurring in a few markets, it has driven price hikes on a global scale. For example, trade energy embargoes on fossil fuels headed for central Europe also increased electricity costs in northern Europe. Due to the interconnection of ecosystems, cascading impacts become broader than the initial cause and could jeopardize some of the Sustainable Development Goals (SDG), such as SDG 7—affordable and clean energy.

Resilience is a term used within the business community and academia, often with various meanings. It commonly refers to the ability to bounce back and return to a previous state after a disturbance. In the context of enterprises, the term describes the ability to maintain core capabilities, identity, and structure, and the capacity for agile transformation. For an organization to be resilient, it thus needs to be capable of handling systemic disruptions that can be random, accidental, or even intentional.

Living in an uncertain world where ecosystems grow in number and complexity brings into focus ways to deal with, survive, and even evolve around disruptive events. Recent world events such as the pandemic and its consequences on businesses have intensified discussions on disruptive changes, risk management, and other means of strengthening resilience.

The disruptive events of the past often have had short-term business impacts as leaders seek to return to a state of normalcy. However, we are now in an era of cumulative and extreme disruption that should more sustainably change future decision making. For example, some immediate consequences of the war in Ukraine could be medium- to long-term sanctions and countersanctions, commodity shortages, and supply chain disruption—so companies need to factor them in as part of their agenda.

Defining Crisis and Crisis Management

A crisis is defined as an event whose occurrence is highly improbable but has drastic consequences necessitating swift and precise action. The crisis event is often ambiguous, with evolving circumstances.

A crisis is fundamentally different from an emergency. Emergency often refers to "a complex and urgent, but also a routine problem." Fires, hostage-taking, and traffic accidents are *routine emergencies*, and trained emergency responders are expected to manage the situation and restore order. Crises push institutions to their limits and established routines as well as day-to-day standard operating procedures can no longer apply, requiring adaptation and improvisation.

From this author's perspective, a crisis can be defined as follows:

A damaging event or series of events that are generally characterized by a profound change with a high degree of instability and carries the potential for extreme impact on the organization's sustainability and continuity. It's significant because the damage that can be caused can be physical, financial, or reputational in its scope, and consequently, it will be decisive in determining the future of the organization. (Bawany 2023)

Some crises strike suddenly, while others snowball over some time; they can originate from many sources and take on different forms. To provide a better understanding of crises, researchers have proposed several ways of categorizing them.

Whereas risk management is traditionally a proactive discipline, crisis management is reactive. Crisis management can be viewed as a specialized discipline within risk management, where specific practices are instituted in response to unexpected events that threaten a company's stability. Having an effective plan and resources mitigates reactivity's destructive nature.

Crisis management is one of several interrelated core disciplines comprising enterprise risk management, along with emergency preparedness, disaster response, business continuity planning, supply chain risk mitigation, and cyber liability prevention. Crisis management practices can help lessen the magnitude of emergencies and disasters while decreasing the uncertainty and anxiety associated with these events.

The management of shocks and crises is becoming an everyday occurrence. Organizations also need to be agile, leverage opportunities, and drive innovation to remain competitive in the face of challenging conditions.

Effective leadership, even under general and everyday circumstances, can be challenging. However, crises pose specific and high-stakes threats to organizations. Crises can yield catastrophic effects on society, the environment, and countless individuals, not to mention threaten an organization's entire existence (Fink 1986). Organizational crisis has been defined as "an event perceived by managers and stakeholders to be highly salient, unexpected, and potentially disruptive" (Bundy et al. 2017, 1663). They manifest in many forms and their intensity may vary by an organization's ability to systematically prepare. Regardless, they all require a response. However, most leaders have not been trained or prepared for all crises—yet still, organizations must rely on their leaders to demonstrate effectiveness and show the way forward from a crisis' onset to recovery.

The problem with the term *crisis* is that it is used in different ways by different professions. In a general sense, the term implies an undesirable and unexpected situation that poses latent harm to people, organizations, or society and could be viewed as an abnormal event.

Although crises typically engender a sense of urgency, countless chronic crises pose long-term risks that are not urgent in that they do not pose an immediate danger. Climate change, for one, dismisses this definition.

The Harvard Business School definition states that a crisis is:

> *a change—either sudden or evolving—that results in an urgent problem that must be addressed immediately.* (Luecke and Barton 2004)

The word itself originates from the Greek *krisis,* which means *to sift or separate* (Klann 2003). A crisis has the potential to divide an organization's past from its future, to replace security with insecurity, and to separate effective leaders from ineffective ones. A crisis also has the potential to swap routine for creativity and to shift an organization from *business as usual* into significant change.

Like leadership, this term has ancient roots and is well understood. The Chinese defined it in the way they wrote it. Many crisis authors have spoken of how the word *crisis* is composed of two characters (危机 wēi jī), one meaning *danger* and the other *opportunity*. However, it has been convincingly argued that the meaning of wēi jī may not be construed from a strict dictionary interpretation due to the complex nature of interpreting different combinations of Chinese characters (Mair 2007). Although simple Chinese dictionaries show that the word jī has only a couple of meanings, it can acquire hundreds of meanings when it is used in combination with other characters. Thus, the only possible interpretation of wēi jī is *danger + incipient moment/crucial point*. In other words, wēi jī refers to a potentially dangerous situation when something begins or changes.

Despite the failure to associate the word *opportunity* with wēi jī, the fact remains that crises can produce remarkably positive outcomes. It has been said that virtually every crisis contains the seeds of success as well as the roots of failure and that crises contain an element of duality. The basic physics concept that every force has an equal and opposing force appears to apply here since some people always manage to benefit from the sufferings of others. Potential opportunities that can arise from a crisis extend far beyond the simple dictionary definition of opportunity and demonstrate that failure to consider this aspect of crises is not advisable. It is thus telling and disappointing that the crisis gurus quoted above have elected to focus solely on danger and have failed to include opportunity in their definitions.

Conclusion

The last several years is proof of that. As soon as one industry-wide or global crisis is over, another one will take its place. As the world is becoming more connected, it also seems to be getting more complicated—and this constant state of flux is making leadership in business more difficult than ever.

These crises and challenges can be characterized as both "polycrisis" (a confluence of multiple interconnected crises) and "permacrisis" (a prolonged state of crisis) which are all taking place within the context of global instability, fragmentation, and polarisation, with war as a means of politics returning and 'my country first' becoming a strong political feature in many parts of the world, despite the need to tackle the common global challenges we face.

Effective crisis leadership can rescue an organization from chaos and deliver opportunities where before there were only disadvantages. Organizations that successfully handle crises can come out of them stronger and with greater employee, customer, and community loyalty than existed before the crisis. Leaders must look deep into the crisis for opportunities that not only benefit the organization but also raise the potential for individual achievement among the organization's employees. In their search, they should look to human elements—the emotions, the behaviors, and the reactions that affect and are affected by the crisis and can influence its outcome.

CHAPTER 2

The "C.R.I.S.I.S." Leader

The level of disruption that leaders are facing in recent years is unprecedented. The complexity and scale of the disruptive challenges they are navigating have left many leaders feeling overwhelmed.

1. How can an organization not only survive but also evolve and thrive during times of crises and disruptive changes?
2. What is the role of disruptive and innovative technology (including digitalization, GenAI, Metaverse, blockchain computing, etc.) and society in this context?
3. What are the differences between resilience and agility and why are they important?
4. How do organizations balance between mitigating risks and sustainability during these disruptive events and crises?

To answer these questions, the Disruptive Leadership Institute (DLI) interviewed 529 CEOs and C-Suite leaders globally across all industry segments. The research has reaffirmed that not all leaders are struggling (Bawany 2023). Some do thrive in times of crisis and chaos. These leaders who are thriving are not doing so by chance. They are proactively demonstrating specific leadership practices and skills resulting in success for their respective teams and organizations, which will be further elaborated on later.

A crisis also tends to bring a high degree of chaos and confusion into an organization. Typically, there is a lack of information precisely when virtually everyone in the organization has a huge emotional need for it. Those involved need to know and understand what happened, why it happened, and how it will impact their futures. Ambiguity is especially potent.

Leadership

It has been argued that the term *leadership* is ambiguous due to its origins in the common vocabulary (Yukl 1989). The earliest written evidence of this originates from Egyptian hieroglyphics dating back to 2300 BC. Most character-based languages have unique symbols for *leader* and *leadership* and do not spell them out. According to one Egyptian scholar, the Pharaoh possessed the quality of a perceptive heart and was endowed with a speech that was characterized by authority and justice (Lichtheim 1973). Similar qualities were enounced by Sun Tzu in 512 BC, who wrote that a leader stands for the virtues of wisdom, sincerity, benevolence, courage, and strictness (Tzu 2005).

Attempts to produce a single unifying definition have repeatedly fallen short of acceptance. Leadership authors like to quote Stogdill who said, "there are almost as many definitions of leadership as there are persons who have attempted to define the concept," but this just states the obvious. The efforts of writers on the ingredients of effective leadership have produced conclusions about what leaders do that are often confusing and even conflicting (Bass and Stogdill 1990). In this climate of disagreement, several descriptions of what makes for effective leadership have gained more favor than others. Among the more widely accepted factors are traits, behavior, information processing, relationships, and follower perceptions (Kets de Vries 2004).

From this author's perspective, leadership can be defined as follows:

The ability of an individual to envision the future and impact and influence the followers toward achieving it by giving purpose (meaningful direction) to the collective effort embodying values and creating the organizational climate where the purpose can be accomplished. (Bawany 2023)

Influence is the ability to persuade, convince, motivate, inspire, and judiciously use power to affect others positively. It's not the kind of authority that comes from leveraging title, position, or regulations. But exactly how is this different from other methods of leadership that managers carry out every single day? After all, the ability to influence others is an important part of leadership in good circumstances as well as bad. The power of influence would seem to be a useful leadership skill no matter what the managerial style of the individual leader, where some managers are more participative and coaching than others and some are more coercive or autocratic and pacesetting, for example, in the way they approach their work (Bawany 2023).

The difference lies not in the importance of influence as a leadership capacity but rather in the context of the crisis itself, an emotional cauldron (a situation characterized by instability and strong emotions) that distills the components of influence into a potent concentration of empathy, caring, and empathetic listening and communication. Crisis leadership is a special case in which these specific tools of influence perform a critical role. In a crisis, timelines are more critical. There isn't as much time for reflection. Rapid decision making and a higher call to action become the norm (Bawany 2015a).

Crisis Leadership

Leading in a crisis can be challenging. Managers who have led in such circumstances describe the experience as highly developmental—a benchmark in their professional careers. But what does effective leadership during a crisis look like? There may be as many descriptions of leadership and crisis leadership; however, this author would define crisis leadership as follows:

> *The ability of an individual to recognize uncertain situations or potentially damaging events or series of events that possess latent risks and opportunities to ensure organization preparedness and make and implement critical decisions through influencing followers resulting in successfully eliminating or reducing the threats or negative impact of the said situation or event.* (Bawany 2023)

The "C.R.I.S.I.S." Leader

Effective Leadership Practices in Crisis Response

A crisis creates a series of conditions that test the limits of teams and organizations, often forcing leaders to re-examine their core values. The word *crisis* broadly describes a low-probability event that has a high potential for serious consequences. Crises are time-sensitive, and as the clock ticks, the window to achieve a successful outcome closes. To make matters more challenging, the unexpected and often unprecedented nature of a crisis means that reliable information to assist decision making is scarce. Leaders must grapple with uncertainty surrounding the cause and the solution to the crisis. Considered together, these elements create a tumultuous storm through which leaders must navigate.

To lead effectively during a crisis, it is beneficial to examine how a crisis impacts team dynamics. Given the high degree of uncertainty surrounding a crisis, leaders may feel that they are losing control. Therefore, some may reflexively overcompensate for this loss and attempt to control as many facets of the team as possible. However, this overreliance on centralizing decisions and tasks, instead of delegating, can produce massive inefficiencies in crisis response. Simply put, micromanaging may restore the leader's sense of control at the expense of the team's efficiency, which delays the implementation of effective strategies.

Leaders may also be tempted to switch to a survival mode. In this scenario, all energy and focus are directed toward minimizing the immediate threat, protecting reputation, and cutting costs. Although this leadership mentality can be necessary for the short-term response to a crisis, it may marginalize the emotional needs of the team and the public, who are experiencing panic, isolation, anxiety, and helplessness. In addition, a persistent survival mentality can undermine the team's sense of purpose and long-term mission.

Effective crisis leadership boils down to responding to the human needs, emotions, and behaviors caused by the crisis. Effective leaders respond to those emotional needs as those needs are perceived by those experiencing the crisis, not just to their perception of what those emotional needs are, might be, or should be. The crisis will affect employee morale, attitudes, productivity, ability to focus, stress levels, relationships, and more. People are more apt to follow a leader who is reassuring and who can meet their primary needs—those needs they least want to give up.

The military's single peacetime focus is preparing for combat, the ultimate crisis, because it involves life and death. A major element of the military's training teaches soldiers how to deal with the range of emotions they will experience before, during, and after combat (Klann 2003). These emotions generally include horror, apprehension, grief, rage, revenge, loneliness, sadness, repulsion, vigilance, anguish, and guilt. Military leaders know these emotions will be experienced and must be controlled or the soldiers will not be able to function on the battlefield. Combat leaders must learn to deal with their own emotions as well as with the emotions of the soldiers under their charge. This is the same challenge civilian leaders face during a crisis, and they can expect the same kinds of emotional chaos to flow over the people in their organization and themselves.

Modern crises unfold in front of a worldwide audience because of the rise in the 24-hour news cycle and increased access to media. Therefore, today's leaders must not only contend with the crisis itself but also navigate scrutiny in real time; minute-to-minute updates can make or break public trust. This intense spotlight might tempt leaders to avoid blame and escape accountability for a crisis. These self-interested tendencies can foster an *every man for himself* mentality that sows mistrust among team members. Consequently, the leader's communication style and degree of consistency shape the team's morale and guide public perception of the leader's response.

Crisis researchers recognize that leaders who routinely deliver honest and empathetic communication are most effective during a crisis. Although it is challenging to remain transparent about bad news and setbacks as a crisis develops, the payoff is that the team and the public perceive the leader as authentic. Thus, leaders must avoid downplaying credible threats and overpromising positive outcomes that they know to be unrealistic. In addition, displays of genuine empathy for those affected by the crisis reflect self-awareness and acknowledgment of peripheral stakeholders, not just their immediate organization.

Recognizing that a company faces a crisis is the first thing leaders must do. It is a difficult step, especially during the onset of crises that do not arrive suddenly but grow out of familiar circumstances that mask their nature. Examples of such crises include the Severe Acute Respiratory Syndrome (SARS) outbreak of 2002 to 2003 and the COVID-19 pandemic in 2020 to 2022. Seeing a slow-developing crisis for what it might become requires leaders to overcome the normalcy bias, which can cause them to underestimate both the possibility of a crisis and the impact that it could have.

Corporate crises can be highly damaging. They erode trust, destroy company value, and, for some, can ultimately lead to the organization's failure. However, these impacts are not inevitable outcomes; some organizations and leaders do thrive during a crisis. In the initial research in 2022, the DLI set out to understand why this was the case with a research project delivered in partnership with the Centre for Executive Education, a global executive development organization headquartered out of Singapore (Disruptive Leadership Institute 2022).

The data collection included both qualitative and quantitative analyses as well as in-depth interviews conducted with over 529 C-suite executives (CEOs and their direct reports) around the world (North America; Europe, Middle East, and Africa; and Asia-Pacific). The respondents identified the megatrends of disruptive forces that are expected to impact their organizations in the coming years.

The research also uncovered exemplary leaders who have been able to navigate successfully the organizational and leadership challenges resulting from the COVID-19 pandemic and the past disruptive events including the Global Finance Crisis in 2018 to 2019. These leaders have demonstrated the competencies, behaviors, and traits of a "C.R.I.S.I.S." leader.

The "C.R.I.S.I.S." model (see Figure 2.1) offers a summary of the contemporary research-based leadership practices that are linked with successful crisis response Bawany (2023). Each skill, trait, and

Figure 2.1 The C.R.I.S.I.S. leadership model

perspective is a useful tool for leading during a crisis. But they are even more effective when integrated into a single crisis leadership strategy. Consider how the following skills, traits, and perspectives might add to a leader's ability to get results through others even during times of crisis.

The "C.R.I.S.I.S." Leadership Model

Communicate

Particularly during a crisis, the ability to genuinely and effectively empathize with the people affected can make all the difference regarding whether a leader will succeed or fail. Never have leaders been under such intense scrutiny from their stakeholders aimed at assessing whether they demonstrate the care, authenticity, purpose, and values that organizations profess to subscribe to.

Crisis communications from leaders often hit the wrong notes. Time and again, we see leaders taking an overconfident, upbeat tone in the early stages of a crisis—and raising stakeholders' suspicions about what leaders know and how well they are handling the crisis. Authority figures are also prone to suspend announcements for long stretches while they wait for more facts to emerge and decisions to be made.

Neither approach is reassuring. As Amy Edmondson wrote,

> *Transparency is* job one *for leaders in a crisis. Be clear about what you know, what you don't know, and what you are doing to learn more.* (Edmondson 2020)

Thoughtful, frequent communication shows that leaders are following the situation and adjusting their responses as they learn more. This helps them reassure stakeholders that they are confronting the crisis. Leaders should take special care to see that each audience's concerns, questions, and interests are addressed. Having members of the crisis response team speak firsthand about what they are doing can be particularly effective.

Communications shouldn't stop once the crisis has passed. Offering an optimistic, realistic outlook can have a powerful effect on employees and other stakeholders, inspiring them to support the company's recovery.

The DLI research has found that inspiring and transformational leaders during times of crisis tend to seek out and act on the counsel or advice of others. They also have a team of advisors that can offer as many perspectives as possible on their situation, be it organizational or leadership challenges.

It is never easy to communicate bad news with the inherent risk of unsettling key stakeholders. In the context of a crisis such as COVID, it is tempting to talk down the threat to the organization. However, these leaders owe it to their stakeholders to provide honest depictions of reality and to be as clear as possible about known facts as well as *known unknowns*. Attempts to underplay the threat will undermine the credibility of future communications, as well as the trust that is integral to successful organizational culture.

Aside from dealing with bad news, communication more broadly is a critical aspect of leading during a crisis. It is important to communicate early and frequently, even with incomplete information. Strong public speaking and motivational skills are a vital part of a leader's skill set but these are particularly important in a crisis. Communications must also have some positivity and hope for the future to motivate stakeholders and direct their energy. This may be viewed as bounded optimism.

After seeing Marriott's revenue fall by nearly 75 percent in most markets because of COVID-19, CEO Arne Sorenson wanted to deliver a video message to employees. His team advised against it because of his appearance: He had been undergoing treatment for pancreatic cancer, and chemotherapy had left him bald. Sorenson made the video, nonetheless. In it, he announced that he and the company's chairman would forgo their salaries in 2020 and that the executive team's compensation would be halved. He choked up at the end while talking about supporting Marriott associates around the world (Aten 2020). The video has inspired other leaders to give up their salaries too (Sundheim 2020).

Communicating clearly and often during a crisis is essential but can be difficult. A leader has some advantage if the organization's crisis management action plan has set up some communication guidelines. With or without a guide, however, the bottom line is simple: Keep internal and external communication lines open and working so that everyone is informed, and they don't have to make up their own stories about the crisis.

Based on the seriousness of the crisis (i.e., the perceived level of the crisis), the organization's senior leaders must also decide who should be informed, when, and how. These stakeholders might include the organization's employees, community groups, local government leaders and officials, government regulators, stockholders, customers, suppliers, the local neighborhood, and the news media.

From the outset of the crisis, senior leaders should be out among the employees sharing what they know has occurred, explaining what is being done about it now (and what steps are being taken so it won't happen again), and, when possible, describing implications for the future. Leaving employees out of the information loop during a crisis can be a major mistake. An organization's employees are loud voices for the organization. They will undoubtedly tell their immediate circle of influence what they think happened, based on what they know. Their knowledge can be the truth that they heard from their leaders, or it can be the rumors and gossip they heard in the hallway. If they are not told what is going on, their fears and anxieties about the crisis can turn into anger, distrust, and even revenge. And the organization will become the target of these emotions and possibly destructive behavior.

Many consider New Zealand a success story in its handling of COVID-19. Prime Minister Arden's communication concerning COVID-19 has been exemplary. In the context of the early lockdown, by directing people to *stay home to save lives,* the prime minister succinctly offered real purpose to her direction. While giving direction, this early communication also involved meaning, as Arden was creating a narrative around how New Zealand would work together to overcome the threat of COVID (Friedman 2020). Similarly, the way Arden addressed the nation from home—wearing casual clothes and with a child's toys in plain sight—at a time of national lockdown was a great example of showing empathy and identifying with her citizens (Ardern 2020).

What the organization's leadership initially communicates to the organization's internal and external stakeholders should include (and generally be limited to) the known details of the situation, what went wrong and why, what is being done to deal with the immediate situation, and the actions that are and will be taken to ensure that the situation does not happen again. Leaders should stick to the facts and avoid conjecture. In the early stages of the crisis, it is also wise to avoid speculating about the future implications of the crisis. If pressed, leaders can say that the greater implications are unknown at present but will be analyzed. Under no circumstances should leaders fabricate or change information with the intent to deceive. Such actions will certainly be found and exacerbate the crisis.

There are immediate and specific communication actions that leaders can take to reduce the negative impact of the crisis and sustain (and perhaps even improve) relationships with stakeholders. Some of the most important external stakeholders during a crisis are the media; and clear, consistent communication with them is critical during a crisis. The news media can extend the leader's communication resources. If handled correctly, a leader can use the media to exert a powerful, positive, emotional impact on all stakeholders and on the organization's employees.

The best practices adopted by these leaders include asking themselves the following questions:

- ***Do I have access to diverse voices and sources of information?*** They adopt scenario planning to determine whose knowledge or expertise they might need in various kinds of crises and identify whether their organization currently has access to it.
- ***Do I routinely consider other team members' ideas or feedback when making decisions?*** They sought out expertise to fill their blind spots and make informed decisions. Effective crisis leaders are those who know when—and how—to defer to others.
- ***What systems or processes might I put into place to surface and capture others' perspectives?*** They look at how communication is structured within their organization and whether there are barriers or silos that they need to proactively address.

Resilience

During times of crisis, these thriving leaders remain calm and sustain their energy levels under pressure to cope with and adapt to disruptive changes. They bounce back from setbacks. They also overcome major difficulties without engaging in dysfunctional behavior or harming others. Resilient leaders are genuinely, sincerely empathetic, walking compassionately in the shoes of employees, customers, and their broader ecosystems.

The well-being and resilience of self and others are more important now than ever before. Role modeling around well-being will be important for leadership success as well as the need for clear messaging on psychological first aid, well-being, and mental health from the business.

These leaders in the middle of a crisis are faced with a flurry of urgent issues across what seems like innumerable fronts. Resilient leaders zero in on the most pressing of these, establishing priority areas that can quickly cascade.

An essential focus in a crisis is to recognize the impact the uncertainty is having on the people that drive the organization. The priority should be safeguarding workers, ensuring their immediate health and safety, followed by their economic well-being. At such times, emotional intelligence is critical. In everything they do during a crisis, resilient leaders express empathy and compassion for the human side of the upheaval, for example, acknowledging how radically their employees' priorities have shifted away from work to being concerned about family health, accommodating extended school closures, and absorbing the human angst of life-threatening uncertainty. Resilient leaders also encourage their people to adopt a calm and methodical approach to whatever happens next.

Credibility is a valuable leadership commodity during a crisis. It's built on consistency, but consistency isn't just the ability to do the same thing over and over. It's also the ability to spring back from negative comments and adapt to rapid changes, to be resilient.

Mary Lynn Pulley and Michael Wakefield (2001) write in *Building Resiliency: How to Thrive in Times of Change* that resiliency is important because change is so pervasive. It's hard to imagine change as dramatic as that brought about by chaos, and resiliency creates a continuity of effective leadership around which people in an organization can rally.

Leadership consistency is like the smooth ride of a well-engineered car—the car's suspension system adapts to the bumps in the road to protect the passengers and provide stability. In the same way, a leader who can handle change and difficulty with flexibility, courage, and optimism protects others in the organization, provides stability in a tumultuous environment, and inspires trust.

Resiliency reflects the mental toughness required to keep your leadership on the road and moving forward during the twists and turns of a crisis. During a crisis, leaders at all levels are faced with all kinds of extremely unpleasant possibilities, such as serious injury to themselves or others, the destruction of property and equipment, or worse. They must be resilient and mentally tough enough to handle the situation. There can be no indifference or resignation. When the leader hangs tough, it shows others in the organization that someone cares enough about them and their welfare to take the punishment and to keep springing back. To quit or resign is not an option because it would result in the loss of all influence and credibility.

Agility

While much of the above is self-explanatory, the need for agility when facing future crises is especially important. One positive phenomenon of the crisis has been the speed at which the leaders of many of these organizations have accelerated their uptake of technology, built resilience into their supply chains, and created alternative revenue streams. Some of these changes, such as Unilever shifting from producing skin care products to cleaning and hygiene products, were simply demand-driven. In other cases, these have been to develop or expand online distribution channels and move from B2B to B2C models. While many of these pivots extend existing capacity and are aligned with the organization's strategy, some might be permanent. Importantly, the agile decision making that leads to these shifts needs to be embedded into the organizational DNA as organizations set the path to recovery.

Agility and resiliency are highly correlated concepts, and both are essential for adapting to disruption and times of crisis. It is important to understand that they are not the same, yet they are often confused in management literature and by business leaders and practitioners.

Several decades ago, businesses were built to last. The successful companies were the stable companies—those that consistently, dependably offered a product or service desired by the masses. The goal for those running these businesses was to eliminate uncertainty, complexity, and variability where possible.

Lengthy, tedious planning cycles and bureaucratic processes are hallmarks of this type of business. The uncertainty in complex projects is dealt with by planning experts who would attempt to predetermine every possible detail before implementation. Success is measured by the extent to which the plan is followed and predetermined milestones are achieved. While a traditional approach to business management persists in some types of organizations today, it is often being replaced by a more dynamic, agile approach.

Today, businesses are built to change. Rather than being viewed as problems to eliminate, complexity, uncertainty, and dynamism are seen as inevitable factors involved in meeting the ever-changing customer demands. The most successful organizations are those able to constantly evolve to continuously add value to their customers' lives.

Today's hyper-competitive world can be a tough place for many businesses. Large companies are always looking to produce better products while reducing costs, customers' needs evolve, and the world economy fluctuates greatly. In a sentence, your business will face many threats. But how do you survive?

A successful business knows when to bend, pivot, and change to accommodate forces more powerful than itself, a process that requires *business agility*. Business agility can be used to adjust to market changes in addition to internal business changes.

Business agility refers to the company's ability to quickly adapt to changes and fluctuations in its business environment. The faster a company can adjust its business strategy, the higher its business agility. Business agility is an organizational method to help businesses adapt quickly to market changes that are either external or internal. If a business is set up to respond rapidly and with the flexibility to meet customer demands, they're more likely to thrive and keep those customers.

Resilient organizations are those that rebound and prosper after business disruption because they're adaptive, agile, and sustainable. Resilient organizations have resilient leaders who see change as opportunities for continued growth rather than a source of anxiety and fear. Response, recovery, and contingencies are the basis of resilience.

To achieve organizational high performance in an era of constant disruption and crisis, both *agility and resilience* are important. This author defines both terms as follows:

Agility refers to the ability to make a rapid change and achieve flexibility in various aspects of the operations, in response to changes or disruptive events in the external environment that could be characterized as a volatile, uncertain, complex, ambiguous, and disruptive (VUCAD) environment. It can also be viewed as the capacity for responding with speed and flexibly and decisively toward anticipating, initiating, and taking advantage of opportunities and avoiding any negative consequences of change. (Bawany 2023)

Resilience refers to the ability to anticipate, prepare for, and recover from disasters, emergencies, and other disruptions, and protect and enhance workforce and customer engagement, supply network and financial performance, organizational productivity, and community well-being when disruption occurs. It can also be viewed as the capacity for resisting, absorbing, and responding, even reinventing, if necessary, in response to fast and/or disruptive change that cannot be avoided such as the black swan events. (Bawany 2023)

Leaders should also explore opportunities for developing collective agility where major challenges require entire systems to be agile and adaptable. Such challenges require whole-system collaboration and design rather than piecemeal solutions. The accelerated delivery of COVID-19 vaccines in the United States is an illustration of whole-system design and collaboration across all stakeholders in the system. This ranges from manufacture, regulatory approval, vaccine distribution and tracking, supply chain coordination, and a range of health care systems and pharmacies. There are many advantages to encouraging a horizontal and vertical cross-section of the system to codesign the strategic outcomes as well as the business model and tactics. These include an outside-in perspective, facilitation of buy-in, identifying bottlenecks and problems early, and quicker decision making (Deloitte 2020).

Crisis leaders who demonstrate resilience can withstand shocks, manage complexity, are quick to learn, and are agile enough to recover from tough times or times of crisis. Resilience can be viewed as the speed and strength of one's response to tragedy and adversity. These leaders demonstrate the ability to lead when considerable ambiguity exists about the best way forward. They listen carefully to voices inside and outside the company for new information that might require a change of direction, and they think creatively about new ways of doing things.

They thrive in crises as they can balance their focus between the immediate challenges of a dynamic situation and the need to anticipate midterm disruptions. They are curious about issues that are emerging, in addition to those that have emerged. This might involve running simulations to identify how their business can anticipate potential challenges ahead.

Crisis leaders act decisively and rapidly to institute revised arrangements to prevent business disruption and potential business failure. They don't dwell on failure but rather acknowledge the situation, learn from their mistakes, and move forward.

They can stay focused, productive, and energetic, despite the inevitable chaos and change swirling around them. They are skilled in helping their team to do the same for everyone, as well as the organization, to succeed and thrive.

They have a habit of looking at stress as a challenge to overcome, and this motivates them to address the causes of their stress in positive ways.

This active approach can be contrasted with a more common approach, where stress is viewed as an unfortunate or even paralyzing force that overwhelms rather than motivates.

These leaders accept challenges and work to overcome them and even master them. Even in intractable situations, they would work toward exploring possibilities that do exist and pursue them. They are committed to an active, engaged outlook toward challenges, which motivates them to actively attempt to influence their surroundings and to persevere even when their attempts don't seem to be working out. Resilient people are dedicated to finding that meaning—toward taking an active, problem-solving approach to situations.

Intelligence (Business Intelligence and Data Analytics)

We don't know when or where the next crisis will strike—or what form it will take. The only things we can control are how we prepare for crises and how we respond to them. In both instances, decision analytics plays a critical role.

When *Harvard Business Review* investigated why some companies had reached new levels of success in the years following the Great Recession of 2008 to 2009, the researchers concluded that preparation was the differentiating factor (Gulati, Nohria, and Wohlgezogen 2010).

Crises change markets, industries, and economic processes. Hence the key to success is change management. One of the best ways to manage change is by making wise decisions about debt, workforce management, and new technologies. The best way to improve business decision making is by supporting those decisions with advanced data analytics.

In times of crisis, business intelligence (BI) is an area that leaders can leverage successfully when revenues are decreasing, and budget problems come into play. By leveraging BI and big data analytics, leaders will be able to discover things that are not obvious or that they didn't know, such as the root cause of those revenue drops and how they affect specific levers within their organization.

Data Analytics

Data analytics is an emerging field in the 21st century when using analytical tools has become a fundamental part of the business decision-making process, including operations on crisis management. The exponential growth of data, with technological advancement, inspires the creation of devices such as smartphones and the development of space technologies. As a result, the amount of information generated from these devices and technologies is surging, leading to the so-called big data, which has become a disruptive element in the workforce. Data analytics has been demonstrated to be an asset in identifying patterns, predicting outcomes, and guiding corporate strategies (Ngai, Xiu, and Chau 2009).

Data analytics is a set of analytical and functional tools to gain insights into business processes and uncover hidden patterns from the BI view. It is the use of data obtained from different sources, via statistical and quantitative analysis, explanatory and predictive models, and fact-based management to guide the decision making and activities of the stakeholders (Davenport and Harris 2007). It is a collection of theories and technologies that turn raw data into relevant and usable information for day-to-day operations, based on the analysis of datasets to deduce the information found within them. Some business questions can be answered to find potential prospects that will give a company a competitive edge in the market. These are *What happened?* in a descriptive sense, *Why did it happen?* in a diagnostic sense, and *When might it happen?* in a predictive sense.

Data-driven decision making is observed as an essential part of business operations. It is achieved by extracting descriptive insights to observe current operations, predictive insights to forecast possible future events, and prescriptive insights to execute business strategies. Effective planning is a critical factor for allocating the necessary resources with minimal cost and time. The indicators that are gathered from the computational models are part of the crisis and risk management to be ready for any outcome. These insights can show an upcoming systemic risk, such as allocating resources that will avoid these downturns or delay the losses.

Proper risk management is critical for each company during difficult times. Analytics can be used to manage business continuity and retention by monitoring, forecasting, and preparing for crisis management and incorporating them into the strategy. The decision-making process is an important aspect of business that affects economic development and the long-term viability of the business in the external environment it operates.

The use of business analytics in a data-driven setting shows that there is a way to enhance management capability by offering valuable insights. These observations will pave the way for a good business strategy that puts them ahead of the competition. Because of advancements in information technology, data analytics has enabled service technology systems to create innovative ways to respond to customer needs.

Business Intelligence

BI is a computer-supported system used for identification and to produce new insights and high-quality knowledge to support decision making (Božič and Dimovski 2019). BI is learning from business experience, which explains the behavioral approach to using informatics and information technology to make decisions. It is an important part of organizational planning to gain intuitive sight and to execute the operations phase by phase based on these informal gatherings. Knowledge workers and data scientists are essential for each company to establish its corporate strategy and planning.

BI is a sequence of operational processes to provide the right information in the right format and to represent such information to the consumer in real time. Intelligent decision support systems and knowledge management databases are part of these advanced evolutionary stages. The multilayer framework is promoted by casual interdependencies and the holistic design of business analytics. BI systems' maturity is based on information content quality, information access quality, analytical corporate culture, and the use of information for decision making.

Data analytics can be used to evaluate these risks, known as black swan events, where the value creation would be preserved while focusing on evaluating contingencies that threaten the present business model.

Organizational ambidexterity is the ability to respond to changes in the business environment where each firm may encounter environmental ambiguity, which is defined as instances when business relationships are unclear because of a lack of information. A firm needs to achieve organizational ambidexterity when it faces a competitive environment. This requires companies to recognize new information to adjust dynamic capabilities while focusing on internal and external changes. Dynamic capabilities of the organizations evolve with sensing new opportunities that can influence organizational decision making.

Competitive advantage is derived from a firm's ordinary capabilities that have been transformed through these decision capabilities.

During the DLI research, it was found that the organizations leveraged data analytics to enhance their dynamic strategic capability in corporate planning during these systemic risks and crises. It helps these organizations understand uncertain economic environments to stay competitive, while the focus is on day-to-day operations. Business cycles are directly affected by value creation where the agile frameworks play a factor.

Most organizations have crisis management teams, protocols, and business continuity to guide current actions and forecast possible responses to future events including pandemics and unexpected downturn risks. These policies need to reduce business-critical operations and travel, distribute all critical operations across the departments for effective decision making, diagnose employees at work, or ask them to stay at home if they are sick.

Although the main emphasis is containing and mitigating the risk from these unexpected events themselves, during the COVID-19 pandemic, these companies established a corporate plan for unanticipated business risks and downturns. These actions include updating BI daily, necessitating new strategies of mitigation rather than containment, using experts' knowledge and predictive forecasting understanding of what's happening and will happen including epidemic and public health intelligence, and establishing resilience principles in developing policies that also include consistent communication with the employees and evolvability for preparedness for the next possible crisis. These policies for dealing with and resolving the ability to forecast immediate results are get-ready scenarios for current and future situations. Dealing with and resolving the immediate problems that COVID-19 presents to each company's workforce as well as creating resilience protocols that can foresee similar cyclical events will enable businesses to continue operating throughout this pandemic crisis.

When dealing with black swan events like pandemics, data-driven decision making is a crucial tool, and predictive analytics can foresee similar catastrophes. Crisis management capacities of businesses will need to be more data-driven and based on forecasting technologies to prepare for probable pandemic-like situations.

Black Swan is thought to be a systemic shock to financial markets and daily societal life that may change social standards. Data analytics are used in risk management as part of crisis management, where data-driven decision making is given top importance to control and prevent such disruptions.

Shifting the Mental Model

In a crisis, leaders are compelled to try to implement measures that they have never attempted before. When a leader adopts a growth mindset in a crisis, the path to change tends to be less arduous, as individuals with a growth mindset believe their talents and abilities are developed through self-development and practice. They are open to new ideas and learning and see failures as opportunities.

Believing that your qualities are carved in stone—the *fixed mindset*—creates an urgency to prove yourself over and over. If you have only a certain amount of intelligence, a certain personality, and a certain moral character, then you'd better prove that you have a healthy dose of them. It simply wouldn't do to look or feel deficient in these most basic characteristics (Dweck 2006).

There's another mindset in which these traits are not simply a hand you're dealt and must live with, always trying to convince yourself and others that you have a royal flush when you're secretly worried it's a pair of tens. In this mindset, the hand you're dealt is just the starting point for development. This *growth mindset* is based on the belief that your basic qualities are things you can cultivate through your efforts, your strategies, and help from others. Although people may differ in every way—in their initial talents and aptitudes, interests, or temperaments—everyone can change and grow through application and experience (Dweck 2006).

Those thriving leaders interviewed during the DLI research emphasized the importance of critical thinking, which helps them to establish situational awareness and impose effective strategy, direction, and action in situations that are exceptionally volatile and uncertain. In such circumstances, information available to decision makers is likely to be ambiguous. Also, there may be too much of it or too little, and what there is may appear to be unstructured, confusing, and possibly contradictory.

The situation is likely to be uncertain, and suitable courses of action may not be readily apparent enough to support confident and effective decision making. However, this may be exactly when urgent choices and critical decisions must be made. These leaders recognized these problems as characteristics of crises. They were able to leverage the business of managing information to establish situational awareness. This awareness, when shared with their crisis leadership team and key stakeholders, is the essential basis for effective choices of strategy, direction, and action. Shared situational awareness implies creating and maintaining a common understanding of what is going on, what that means (in terms of its implications), and what it might mean (in terms of reasonable deductions that can be made about future developments).

What Is Critical Thinking?

Critical thinking is an active form of reflection that is deliberate, persistent, and careful. It challenges preconceptions, perceptions, and received wisdom. And it is, most important of all, focused on deciding what to believe and what to do. It is, therefore, inherently practical and generates a set of guidelines for the practitioner. It involves what some have called metacognition or the act of thinking about how we think.

Critical thinking aims to better understand the meaning and implications of information, conclusions, options, and decisions and to identify and evaluate the assumptions upon which thinking (our own and others') is based. It can bring a powerful rigor to crisis management if it is applied with perseverance, determination, and self-awareness.

Critical thinking in business literature is often confused with skills like *problem solving*. *Problem solving* is quite different from *critical thinking*.

Sometimes problem solving requires thinking skills, like how best to balance profit and loss statements, but not critical thinking skills —rational, reflective thinking. Some business-related problems, for example, require emotional intelligence, which is thinking that is neither rational nor reflective.

In other words, while critical thinking often refers to *problem solving,* not all problem solving is an example of critical thinking. Critical thinking consists more of *habits of mind* providing a framework in which problem solving can occur. Often, these distinctions aren't clear in business education literature.

How and why is critical thinking applied in the workplace? Critical thinking in the workplace comes in many forms. We see critical thinking being used in teams to help effectively resolve problems. We even see critical thinking being used in the workplace to help teams figure out what issues exist, and then we see teams come up with possible answers for those issues.

Critical thinking is applied to leadership approaches because leaders need to have critical thinking skills, be able to understand logical relationships between ideas, recognize the importance and the relationship of an argument, as well as recognize mistakes in reasoning, and then be able to make the right decisions.

The need for critical thinking in leadership has always been around. A model was developed in 1925, called the Watson–Glaser critical thinking model, which helps organizations identify factors in people that are important for critical thinking and judgmentmaking,

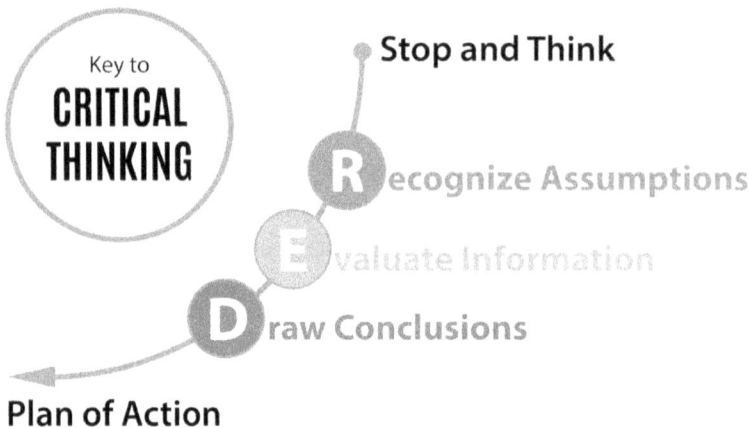

Key to
**CRITICAL
THINKING**

Stop and Think

Recognize Assumptions

Evaluate Information

Draw Conclusions

Plan of Action

Figure 2.2 The RED model of critical thinking

which explains why critical thinking needs to be a part of leadership approaches.

Pearson has developed the following RED model—Recognize assumptions, Evaluate arguments, and Draw conclusions (see Figure 2.2)—as a way to view and apply critical thinking principles when faced with a decision (Chartrand, Ishikawa, and Flander 2018).

Recognize Assumptions

This is the ability to separate fact from opinion. It is deceptively easy to listen to a comment or presentation and assume the information presented is true even though no evidence was given to back it up. Perhaps the speaker is particularly credible or trustworthy or the information makes sense or matches our own view. We just don't question it. Noticing and questioning assumptions helps to reveal information gaps or unfounded logic. Taking it a step further, when we examine assumptions through the eyes of different people (e.g., the viewpoint of different stakeholders), the result is a richer perspective on a topic.

Why does it matter?   This is the ability to separate fact from opinion. It is deceptively easy to listen to a comment or presentation and assume the information presented is true even though no evidence was given to back it up. Noticing and questioning assumptions helps to reveal information gaps or unfounded logic. Taking it a step further, when we examine assumptions through the eyes of different people (e.g., the viewpoint of different stakeholders) the result is a richer perspective on a topic.

How/when to use it.   When you're gathering information, listening to what people say, or assessing a situation, think about what assumptions you have going in. Perhaps you assume that a trusted co-worker is providing reliable information, but is there really evidence to back it up? Learn to see gaps in logic and opinion disguised as fact.

Evaluate arguments

It is difficult to suspend judgment systematically and walk through various arguments and information with the impartiality of Sherlock Holmes. The art of evaluating arguments entails analyzing information objectively and accurately, questioning the quality of supporting evidence, and understanding how emotion influences the situation. Common barriers include confirmation bias, which is the tendency to seek out and agree with the information that is consistent with your point of view or allow emotions—yours or others—to get in the way of objective evaluation. People may quickly conclude simply to avoid conflict. Being able to remain objective and sort through the validity of different positions helps people draw more accurate conclusions.

Why does it matter? We often have problems sorting through conflicting information because we unknowingly let our emotions or pride get in the way or because we only hear what we want to hear (confirmation bias). Being able to remain objective and sort through the validity of different positions helps people draw more accurate conclusions.

How/when to use it. The art of evaluating arguments entails analyzing information objectively and accurately, questioning the quality of supporting evidence, and understanding how emotions—yours or others—influence the situation or get in the way of objectivity. People may quickly conclude simply to avoid conflict. Learn how to push all that aside and analyze information accurately and objectively.

Draw conclusions

People who possess these skills can bring diverse information together to arrive at conclusions that logically follow from the available evidence, and they do not inappropriately generalize beyond the evidence. Furthermore, they will change their position when the evidence warrants doing so. They are often characterized as having *good judgment* because they typically arrive at a quality decision.

Why does it matter?   People who possess this skill can bring diverse information together to arrive at conclusions that logically follow from the available evidence, and they do not inappropriately generalize beyond that evidence. Furthermore, they will change their position when the evidence warrants doing so. They are often characterized as having *good judgment* because of their quality decisions.

How/when to use it.   This is the payoff. When you think critically, the true picture becomes clear, and you can make tough decisions or attack the difficult problem.

Each of these critical thinking skills fits together in a process that is both fluid and sequential.

When presented with information, people typically alternate between recognizing assumptions and evaluating arguments. Critical thinking is sequential in that recognizing faulty assumptions or weak arguments improves the likelihood of reaching an appropriate conclusion. It is helpful to focus on each of the RED skills individually when practicing skill development. With concentrated practice over time, typically several months, critical thinking skills can be significantly increased.

Disruptive Mental Agility—Cognitive Readiness

Mental agility—they are excellent critical thinkers who are comfortable with complexity, scrutinize problems, and make new connections.

The suite of cognitive readiness skills can be viewed as part of the advanced thinking skills that make leaders ready to confront whatever new and complex problems they might face. Cognitive readiness is the mental preparation that leaders develop so that they, and their teams, are prepared to face the ongoing dynamic, ill-defined, and unpredict-

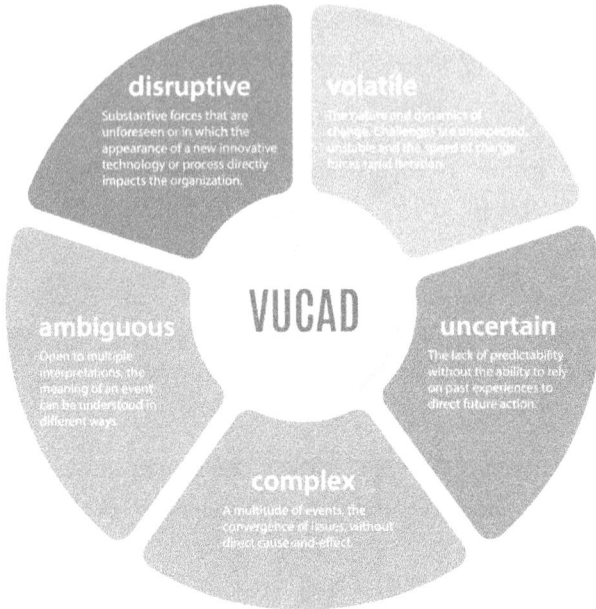

Figure 2.3 Leading in a "VUCAD" world

able challenges in the volatile, uncertain, complex, ambiguous, and disruptive (VUCAD)-driven business environment.

The development of disruptive mental agility will include the suite of cognitive readiness and critical thinking skills. These crucial leadership skills will develop, enhance, or sustain a leader's ability to navigate successfully in this new normal of the VUCAD (see Figure 2.3) business environment and workplace.

The Executive Development Associates (EDA) have identified the following seven key cognitive readiness skills, collectively known as Paragon[7] (Figure 2.4), which will develop, enhance, or sustain a leader's ability to navigate successfully in this new normal (Bawany 2023):

1. Mental cognition: Recognize and regulate your thoughts and emotions.
2. Attentional control: Manage and focus your attention.
3. Sensemaking: Connect the dots and see the bigger picture.
4. Intuition: Check your gut, but don't let it rule your mind.

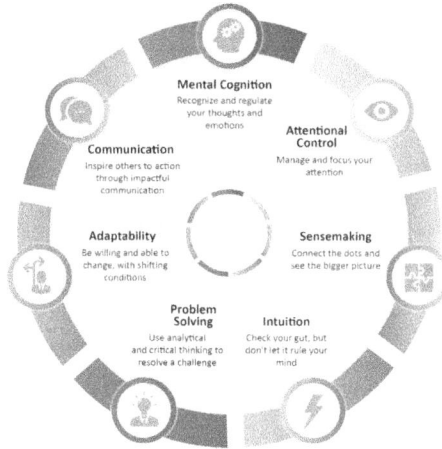

Figure 2.4 Paragon[7] cognitive readiness competencies framework

5. Problem solving: Use analytical and creative methods to resolve a challenge.

6. Adaptability: Be willing and able to change, with shifting conditions.

7. Communication: Inspire others to action; create fluid communication pathways.

The detailed descriptors of each of these seven cognitive readiness competencies can be found in Table 2.1.

Overall, heightened cognitive readiness allows leaders to maintain a better sense of self-control in stressful situations, which is crucial when resolving complex problems and decision making.

Inspiring

During crises, leaders need to demonstrate inspirational and transformational leadership styles. Trust is more valuable than ever during times of crisis because it not only promotes resilience in the face of uncertainty but also provides solid ground for action and results in better financial performance. When leaders and organizations are centered on an authentic purpose, employees feel that their work has meaning.

Employees' trust in their organization is vital during crises and disruptions. It powerfully facilitates employees' ability to respond

Table 2.1 Descriptors of Paragon[7] cognitive readiness competencies

Metacognition	Attentional control	Sensemaking
Metacognition is monitoring and managing your emotional and mental processes. Metacognition comes from the words *meta* meaning beyond and *cognition* meaning thinking. It describes the ability to control your mental and emotional processes and, in turn, manage behaviors and maximize performance. Metacognition involves self-awareness and the use of intentional strategies to self-regulate your cognition, emotions, and actions. Metacognitive individuals and organizations engage in reflective practice. They take time to plan before, during, and after situations.	Attentional control (*mindfulness*) is the skill of actively managing your attention as a finite resource. Attentional control, or mindfulness, is the conscious control of your own attention. People or organizations with high levels of attentional control pick up on weak signals. They can direct and sustain their attention deliberately, without being diverted by distractions, and they can stay focused, even if that sustained attention becomes unpleasant. You can help develop your attentional control *muscles* by practicing attentional shifting and focusing exercises.	Sensemaking is the ability to quickly connect the dots to gain understanding. Sensemaking is pattern-based reasoning; in other words, it's the process of developing an understanding of an event or situation, particularly when it's complex and you lack clear, complete, and orderly data. Good sensemakers *put the pieces together* quickly and overcome information gaps. They discern meaning from patterns and recognize how parts of a system fit into the bigger picture, how individual elements interact, and how short-term goals impact long-term strategies.

constructively to crises and change, and it underpins organizational agility and resilience. Yet it is during such episodes that trust is most threatened. During the COVID-19 pandemic, this conundrum has organizational leaders asking: How can we preserve employee trust in the face of the financial and other challenges posed by the outbreak?

Yet it is during crises and disruption—when trust is most required —that it is also more likely to be lost. The COVID-19 pandemic is posing just such a threat. It requires organizational leaders and policymakers to make rapid, large-scale changes to both sustain organizational viability and maintain the flexibility and ability to later scale up and rapidly return to their core business once the pandemic passes. To ensure organizational survival, they must make tough and

Intuition	Problem solving	Adaptability	Communication
Intuition comes from your *fast thinking* (elephant) cognitive system. Intuition is fast; our minds quickly generate intuitive judgments without active deliberation. We all use intuition—especially under VUCA conditions—but our intuition isn't always reliable. It's important to know when it can be trusted and how to best use it.	Problem solving is an analytical approach to resolving difficult issues. Problem-solving relies upon three factors: subject-matter knowledge, motivation, and problem solving *meta-skill,* which is a mental list of problem-solving techniques and decision strategies typically associated with critical thinking and decision analysis tools.	Adaptability is the ability and willingness to change with shifting conditions. Adaptability is the consistent willingness and ability to alter attitudes, thoughts, and behaviors to appropriately respond to the actual or anticipated change in the environment. This includes flexibility, resilience, responsiveness, and agility.	Communication is about conveying deeper intent and understanding. Communication is the conveyance of information and sentiments. Clear, honest, and frequent communication facilitates team performance. Beyond that, you can use linguistic tools to help increase saliency, clarity, relevance, and persuasive value.

unpopular decisions, such as cutting pay and work hours and laying off workers temporarily or permanently. The uncertainty and unpredictability of the pandemic have jolted employees out of their familiar ways, including their habitual trust in their employers, and have heightened their sense of vulnerability. In such a context, employees need and seek reassurance from their employer that their continued trust is deserved.

Leaders must take key practical actions to preserve trust. The DLI research shows that during crises, employee trust can not only be preserved but also be enhanced. These thriving leaders show that employees who feel a greater sense of connection are far more likely to ride out volatility and be available to help companies recover and grow when stability returns.

Central to reducing uncertainty is drawing on and reinforcing the familiar, established foundations of trust that already exist in the organization. These trust foundations are unique to each organization and include the values, purpose, relationships, practices, organizational structures, and processes that built and sustained employee trust before the crisis. For example, in one government agency we studied, trust was founded strongly on principles of fairness, integrity, and professional respect. In a manufacturing business, employee trust was based on a unionized culture and the strong relationships between line managers, workers, and trade unions at the local plant level. These trust foundations highlight what the organization needs to protect and continue to do to preserve employees' trust.

We believe that all leaders can be inspirational during times of crisis as all they need to do is unlock their inspirational potential and find an opportunity to demonstrate their capability. They need to develop the relevant skills that they can learn, grow, and develop to increase their impact and influence on their followers. It is important to understand from the start that becoming an inspirational leader requires focused effort, practice, and the ability to conduct self-reflection. Inspiration is personal; our source of inspiration is closely linked to our beliefs, values, and identity.

Inspirational leadership is both a mindset and a skill. It should be thought of as an action-orientated mindset where one individual can ignite a fire in another person's heart and/or mind and move a person or team of people to act and achieve something greater than the current status quo. Inspirational leadership, at its core, is about finding ways to enhance the potential of those you lead in a way that works for them and inspiring others to push themselves, achieve more, and reach that potential. The methods by which this is done will vary from person to person, and business to business, but the outcome is always the same: People develop greater confidence in what they can do and apply this confidence in a way that benefits the organization they work for.

During times of crisis, when employees aren't just engaged, but inspired, that's when organizations see real breakthroughs. Inspired employees are themselves far more productive and, in turn, inspire those around them to strive for greater heights. The DLI research shows that while anyone can become an inspiring leader as it is believed that they're made, not born, in most companies, there are far too few of them. Those thriving leaders are inspiring as they leverage effectively their unique combination of strengths to motivate individuals and teams to take on bold missions—and hold them accountable for results. And they unlock higher performance through empowerment, not command and control.

While the research found that leaders who inspire are incredibly diverse, which underscores the need to find inspirational leaders who are right to motivate your organization, there is no universal archetype. A corollary of this finding is that anyone can become an inspirational leader by focusing on his or her strengths. Although DLI found that many different attributes help leaders inspire people, it also identified that there is one common trait that matters more than any other: mindfulness. This enables the leaders to remain calm under stress, empathize, listen deeply, and remain present.

Often, leaders have been identified as possessing a remarkable quality that sets them apart from others. It enabled them to have a powerful influence on others. It caused others to be attracted to them and enabled them to achieve remarkable outcomes. That quality has most frequently been labeled *charisma,* a term coming from the Greek word meaning *gift.* In ancient times, it was believed that this quality was indeed a divine gift that was bestowed upon some and not others. The practical consequence of this has been that unlike other leadership skills, such as being results-focused, giving compelling oral presentations, or delegating, no one attempted to teach charisma.

Because the popular press often describes leaders as charismatic, this characteristic has then been used to explain this person's success. The probable reason is that many leaders fell into the seemingly logical trap of thinking that charisma, as the term was most often used, was simply a synonym for being inspiring. There were instances where countless leaders were identified by their colleagues as being highly inspiring and not charismatic. Conversely, some people are seen as quite charismatic and fail to meet the test of being inspiring and motivating—especially in the long run.

Some believe that inspiration is just something that leaders do on big occasions. They see it as that yearly speech where leaders get up in front of all the employees and get them all revved up and inspired. Inspiration is much more than this. The DLI research found that during the recent pandemic, everything a leader does every day has an impact on the employees. When a leader comes to work in the morning and is in a bad mood, that counts. When a leader comes in and shares with colleagues his or her optimism, excitement, and passion for the work, that counts. When a leader comes in, ducks into his or her office, and hides in his or her cave all day, that counts. But if a leader will just take a few minutes to go around and ask people how they're doing, thank them, and encourage them to do more, that counts. Everything leaders do counts. Everything every employee does on every level counts.

Inspirational leadership builds on inspirational appeals. It is probably the most powerful form of leadership and may well be the only soft approach that is scalable and that allows firms to thrive in situations characterized by ambiguity, complexity, and rapid change.

Structure the Recover Plan

A crisis may end, but it doesn't just fade away. Leaders can take several important and influential actions to ensure their organization, and its employees, not only recover but also prepare for a future crisis.

One of the biggest questions employees have asked their leaders during the COVID-19 pandemic is when this coronavirus madness will end so that they can get back to normal or business as usual. The reality is that it is going to be business as unusual. To prepare for the *new normal* or the *next normal,* leaders need to answer the question "What can I do now to prepare for when things return to a new normal?" To achieve this, they need to reflect on what has happened and what lessons they have learned and then plan to start with a new vision.

They need to connect the conversation about why they and the leadership team are embarking on preparing the organization for the future, what the outcomes are likely to be, and how to go about it. Leaders need to stay firmly grounded in questions like What's our goal here? What does success look like for us?" Leaders need to build a culture of accountability, foresight, a "people-first ahead of process and technology" mantra, and decisive adaptability. For many organizations, this means asking their workforce to work from home. If you are preparing for increased remote work, ensure that the organization has in place the right technology and the technical capacity to support it, including bandwidth, VPN infrastructure, authentication, access control mechanisms, and cybersecurity tools that can support peak traffic demands. Many leaders have confessed that their organizations were not ready for this!

Reshaping the Organization for Recovery

Two important goals of leadership following a crisis are to rebuild and strengthen relationships (between the people in the organization and between the people and the organization) and to learn from the experience to prepare for the next crisis. In working toward those goals, one of the most effective things leaders can do after the crisis is to assure employees that the probability of the same crisis reoccurring is virtually nonexistent. Otherwise, anxiety levels will remain high in the organization and significantly impact morale and productivity. Leaders at all levels should talk to employees and personally share what preventive measures are being taken to avert another crisis. This allows the employees to ask questions, an act that can be therapeutic and calming.

Another more formal but particularly effective means of providing such reassurance is through updated and highly publicized company rules and regulations aimed at preventing a similar crisis. These revised rules can outline improved crisis assessment procedures, including early

Figure 2.5 Goldman situational leadership styles framework

warning and detection, crisis indicators, and improved interpersonal communication methods among leaders and employees in general.

These assurances can be the first step in rebuilding and reviewing the organization's communication strategies. Clear and continuing communication is as essential after a crisis as it is before and during a crisis. Making sure those lines are open after a crisis helps leaders and the organization to learn from their experience and enhance their capability to deal with future crises. It also helps employees connect to the organization and connect and strengthen the bonds they developed during the crisis.

Demonstrate Transformational and Authoritative (Visionary) Leadership Style

As signs of recovery tentatively creep back into the economy, forward-looking organizations are working to redefine their *business as usual* and arrive at a transformational strategy. Along the way, according to the DLI research, there are important aspects that these thriving leaders take into consideration in charting the way forward.

During the height of the pandemic, most organizations operated in crisis mode. As the world moves toward a postpandemic recovery, these thriving leaders guided their organizations out of emergency mode into something of a semblance of normality. Yet, they are mindful that the crisis remains in the background. Supply chains remain overstretched, and work restrictions continue. So, it's still important to steer organizations on a transformational journey.

The concept of applying and adopting various leadership styles was popularized by psychologist Daniel Goleman through his evidence-based research on emotional intelligence. In his book *Primal Leadership: Realizing the Power of Emotional Intelligence*, Goleman describes six different styles of leadership (see Figure 2.5)—visionary, coaching, affiliative, democratic, pacesetting, and commanding (Goleman 2002) —and how the most effective leaders embrace all six styles, utilizing the appropriate style based on situational, organizational, or human cues (Goleman 2000).

Goleman describes the situation most appropriate for applying visionary leadership as one of directional change, where openness is critical for blazing new paths: "Visionary leaders articulate where a group is going, but not how it will get there—setting people free to innovate, experiment, take calculated risks."

However, when the visionary style is your only style, it can leave your team confused about their priorities, searching for vital details, dealing with *organizational whiplash* in the face of constant change, and unsure where the organization (and their career) is going.

Therefore, it can be critical for visionary leaders to balance their style and surround themselves with fellow C-levels, directors, managers, or team leads more adept at integrating the other leadership styles into the mix when being democratic, coaching, or a pacesetter isn't their strong suit.

Importance of Authoritative Leadership During Crises

Authoritative leaders, also called visionary leaders, tend to approach leadership like a mentor guiding a mentee. Instead of telling their team to follow instructions and do as they say, authoritative leaders put themselves in the scenario and utilize a *come with me* approach. They have a firm understanding of the challenges to overcome and the goals to reach and have a clear vision for achieving success.

Authoritative leaders inspire motivation. They offer direction, guidance, and feedback to maintain enthusiasm and a sense of accomplishment throughout the crisis or business challenge.

At its heart, authoritative leadership depends on a thoroughly developed sense of emotional intelligence. To be effective, authoritative leaders must demonstrate certain emotional intelligence competencies, such as:

1. *Self-confidence*: to develop a vision and inspire others to follow it. Authoritative leaders provide direction and vision. They approach resolving challenges arising from the crisis from a position of confidence. They have a clear vision of what success

looks like and give their team members clear direction and constructive feedback as they work toward achieving those organizational goals.

2. *Empathy and empathetic listening*: to understand and anticipate the emotions felt by team members at key junctures during the crisis. Authoritative leaders breed goodwill as for the authoritative leadership style to work, a person must approach his or her team from a position of empathy. By understanding the personal and professional emotions, desires, and worries of a team member, an authoritative leader is better able to identify potential roadblocks to performance and remove them, while simultaneously incentivizing success.

3. *Ability to adapt:* identify and remove barriers to change that may be required for success on the path of recovery from the crisis. Authoritative leaders bring clarity. They are effective because of their ability to inspire, motivate, and influence their team. Often, this motivation stems from their ability to understand a company's strategic goals and communicate them in a way that's easy for employees to follow. When everyone knows what the organization is striving toward, it's easy to ensure everyone is aligned.

Authoritative Versus Authoritarian Leadership

While the terms *authoritative* and *authoritarian* leadership sound similar—and are often used interchangeably—they are very different.

Authoritative leaders guide their teams by example and inspire progression toward a common goal, whereas authoritarian leaders rely on commands and demand compliance without question. Authoritative leaders say, *Come with me*; authoritarian leaders say, *Do what I tell you*. Authoritative leaders view success as something to be shared by the team; authoritarian leaders view success as stemming from themselves.

While authoritarian leadership, also called commanding leadership, is often viewed as a more negative approach, it can be highly effective in the right circumstances, particularly when a company or organization needs firm guidance through a crisis when compliance with the directives of the board or senior leadership team is crucial for the sustainability of the organization.

Conclusion

Ideally, all of us would balance our intellectual, physical, spiritual, and emotional lives all the time. But that's a difficult job, particularly when a crisis creates an imbalance and tips the scale toward the emotional end. This creates a special challenge for managers who must provide leadership to those who are in a state of emotional turmoil.

Occupying a designated leadership position isn't the same thing as being a leader, doesn't provide leadership on its own, and doesn't prove that the person in that position has the skills or knowledge to be an effective leader. There is a significant difference between being a successful leader because specific numbers were achieved and being an effective leader. After all, the numbers were achieved and the continuing support of direct reports is evident. Leaders who view themselves as successful because of position, salary, or longevity, but leave a high body count of former employees bobbing in their wake, are often surprised to find their careers derailed or sidelined. Nothing separates such leaders from their illusions as quickly and sharply as a crisis because it's then they realize they haven't built the skills necessary to lead effectively during such traumatic events.

An organization's senior leadership is key before, during, and after a crisis, and its quality can determine the length, severity, and ultimate consequences of the crisis. Leaders set the tone by their example and conduct during the crisis. By paying attention to the components of influence (especially communication, empathy, and caring), leaders can have a significant positive impact on the very human, emotionally charged climate that accompanies a crisis. That, in turn, can reduce the negative impact and duration of a crisis for the benefit of the organization.

Effective leaders often have a well-developed ability to influence others and can avoid using authoritarian or fearful tactics to get results. This is an especially important capability in a crisis when strong leadership is essential, and getting results through others using threats, pressure, and coercion is generally unproductive and can even be harmful. Influencing techniques that are effective during normal times become even more critical during a crisis. Because influencing skills are applicable during normal business situations as well as in a crisis, leaders can develop these skills before the heat of a crisis is upon them.

If your day-to-day leadership doesn't bolster trust, garner respect, inspire confidence, and connect emotionally with your direct reports, it's highly improbable that your leadership will dramatically change just because a crisis is at hand.

Authoritative leadership can be particularly well suited for businesses undergoing a period of struggle or change. A department or team not meeting its goals in recent quarters; a shift in company ownership, leadership, or structure; a corporate turnaround after a decline; or a desire to innovate and change organizationally can all be appropriate situations for an authoritative approach.

It isn't, however, applicable to all business challenges. Skilled leaders can tailor their leadership style to whatever scenario they find themselves in.

CHAPTER 3

Crisis Management Planning and Strategy

As the business community has learned through the COVID-19 pandemic, it's more important than ever for leaders to anticipate and plan for the possibility of an unplanned event. The more prepared you are to manage shocks, the less likely you'll fall victim to the serious harm a crisis has the potential to inflict.

Whereas risk management is traditionally a proactive discipline, crisis management (CM) is reactive.

Crisis management (CM) can be viewed as a specialized discipline within risk management, where specific practices are instituted in response to unexpected events that threaten a company's stability. Having an effective plan and resources mitigates reactivity's destructive nature. (Bawany 2023)

To respond to ongoing uncertainty and change, businesses need to embrace a core set of capabilities and behaviors to embed agility and resilience. They need to go beyond their usual business analysis and think about a broader set of future scenarios; they need to plan not just for business as usual, but for any major disruptions that might affect them or a competitor, and they need to be able to act with agility to quickly counter existential threats and take advantage of new opportunities.

To succeed, CEOs and business leaders need to have *adaptability*—the ability to change—and *agility*—the speed of response. This includes both planning for whatever can go wrong and setting up a structure to respond quickly.

To do this, companies need to utilize a range of information and tools to gain insight into their current operations, performance, and market environment and plan for different future environments. These include external insights, such as third-party data and dynamic analytics that can quickly process real-time data and help shape insights into customer demands or concerns.

Scenario planning that utilizes data to help simulate how a company can be impacted by a host of situations, such as a market crash or a product recall, is another key activity. For example, many organizations have built cross-functional teams to look at potential scenarios and be ready to act once the way forward is clear.

To be adaptive and agile, people across different functions of a company need to be empowered to make the decisions to quickly execute change to meet any situation.

This starts with inclusive leadership from the top, which delegates rather than controls, and actively invites input from all levels and can be seen as taking appropriate action based on this input. The traditional top-down structure is likely to be too slow to respond to a threat in today's environment. A key step in change management is to ensure that people feel empowered, are more aware, and are likely to communicate early signs of disruption.

This is also a good time to make sure business units are sharing data, rather than keeping it in silos, to make sure all decision makers can act based on a full set of information.

Boards and leadership teams also need to make sure they have the right leaders in place, with the right skill sets for all situations. An organization may have the best leaders for a growth scenario, but these leaders might not be nimble enough in a turnaround situation.

CEOs, CFOs, and the board should regularly evaluate whether the leadership team has the essential skills for all situations. They can then identify which leaders should take point in different scenarios such as CM or operational restructuring.

Organizations face challenges that present varying levels of severity. But handled poorly, even a seemingly minor shock has the potential to escalate into a crisis that threatens the viability of a business. A crisis can disrupt operations, damage reputations, destroy shareholder value, and trigger other threats.

The media continues to be filled with stories about companies that fail to manage crises, costing them millions in damage, fines, reparations, lost revenue, and lost jobs.

Many of those failures can be tracked to a few common causes:

1. lack of attention to the identification and assessment of risks;
2. weak leadership commitment to effective risk mitigation and CM;
3. no crisis communication plan;
4. no process to assess, investigate, and mitigate a crisis.

As part of an effective enterprise risk management (ERM) program, leaders need to make the right moves when a crisis occurs to resolve the issue and protect the organization.

The following *five steps,* when taken with care and commitment from the board of directors on down, can help ensure the enterprise is well prepared to protect itself when a crisis occurs.

Step 1: Establish a Crisis Management Committee to Evaluate Corporate Governance, Risk Management, and Internal Controls

The Crisis Management Committee will need to have clear *Terms of Reference* which include its goal, the authority of the committee, objectives and outcome measures, in/out of scope, whom to involve, role/responsibilities, frequency of meetings and ways of working, and so on.

Organizations must commit to a regular evaluation of their corporate governance, risk management practices, and internal controls. When addressed together, these three components provide the pillars for a strong CM program. Through a regular review of these pillars of effective governance, corporations can identify new and emerging risks, assess existing risks, and make the policy and process changes needed to address the behaviors that could lead to significant damage to the enterprise—before they evolve into a crisis.

Step 2: Identify the Most Probable Crises and Assess Their Potential Impact

Several kinds of crises are possible in every organization, including natural disasters, unexpected injury or death of employee or customer, harassment or discrimination, workplace violence, employee malfeasance, cybercrime, white-collar crime, litigation or class action, fraud, mismanagement, and product defects/recalls. Other categories may be unique to the business. An enterprise-wide vulnerability assessment, using clearly defined risk indicators, will help to uncover the kinds of crises for which the organization needs to plan and prepare. Extra attention should be given to those crises that are deemed either highly likely to occur or to have the highest potential impact on the organization.

Step 3: Create and Train a Crisis Management Team

Arguably the most important step in an effective ERM and crisis response program is having the crisis team in place. Internal and external experts should be identified, and roles and responsibilities should be delineated. Regular training and crisis exercises are vital to assuring that the team is prepared to execute important response strategies and tasks. Internal expertise should include senior executive management, operations leaders from key areas, and leaders of compliance, internal audit, corporate communications/PR, human resources, legal, sales, and marketing, among others.

External expertise may be needed to supplement the internal team and should include established relationships with outside providers of PR and communications, and legal and forensic counsel, among others. By having these key vendors in place well in advance, they can get to know the company and its leaders, facilitating better, faster responses when a crisis is declared.

Step 4: Develop and Implement a Crisis Communication Plan

Effective communication response to a crisis has never been more important than in this highly charged age of instant communication. Organizations no longer have the luxury of waiting days to respond when an issue arises.

Crisis Communication Plan

Crisis communication plans act as blueprints for the company in times of crisis so that they can respond immediately.

The crisis communications plan is an important component of a business preparedness program. A business must be able to respond promptly, accurately, and confidently during an emergency in the hours and days that follow.

Effective crisis communication plans include details on not only what to do but how to do it. Policies and processes, chains of command, roles, and responsibilities for communication should be detailed.

Best-practice plans contain quick response guides for the most probable crises identified in the vulnerability assessment, including initial strategy and messaging that has been vetted and preapproved by management and legal.

It is an emergency plan that includes the following steps of communication and future prevention to help prepare and navigate through unexpected crises.

1. The need to communicate is immediate when an emergency occurs. Many different audiences must be reached with information specific to their interests and needs.
2. Many potential audiences will want information during and following an incident; each has its own needs for information. The challenge is to identify potential audiences, determine their need for information, and then identify who within the business is best able to communicate with that audience.

Possible audiences may include but are not limited to the board, senior management, employees, customers, suppliers, government officials, and regulators.

3. Contact information for each audience should be compiled in advance and be accessible during an incident. Existing information such as customer, supplier, and employee contact information may be exportable from existing databases. Include as much information for each contact as possible (e.g., organization name, contact name, business telephone number, mobile/WhatsApp number, fax number, and email address). Lists should be updated regularly and secured.

4. News media will be on the scene or calling to obtain details if the incident is serious. There may be numerous requests for information from local, regional, or national media. The challenge of managing large numbers of requests for information, interviews, and public statements can be overwhelming. Determine in advance who will speak to the media and prepare that spokesperson with talking points, so they can speak clearly and effectively in terms that can be easily understood. Prioritizing requests for information and developing press releases and talking points can assist with the need to communicate quickly and effectively.

5. One of the goals of crisis communication planning is to make sure that messages are consistent. Each audience will seek information that is specific to them during and following an incident. Messages can be prescripted as templates with blanks to be filled in when information is available and tailored to each incident. Prescripted messages can be developed, approved by the management team, and stored on a remotely accessible server for quick editing and release when needed.

6. There initially may be limited information about the incident or its potential impacts. Having a coordinated review and distribution process allows the business to adapt to changing information. As days and weeks go by, this messaging will transition from reacting to the incident to moving toward recovery.

Messaging for each step of this process also can be developed in advance.

7. Spokespersons should be identified and trained. Platforms to monitor media and social media should be implemented well in advance. Companies with operations in multiple countries should make sure that their communication plans address important cultural differences so that they can respond appropriately.

8. Finally, the plan should be exercised and updated at least annually to ensure that it is well integrated with an operational response and business continuity (BC) and recovery plans.

Step 5: Develop a Crisis Response Plan

The CM team needs a written plan to effectively manage the crisis. The plan should address levels of crisis with thresholds for activating the team and implementing the plan. It should identify who will lead the response for each type of crisis. Procedures to assess, investigate, and mitigate the crisis are vital. Operational roles and responsibilities should be detailed, and external support services identified and engaged.

As the business community has learned through the COVID-19 pandemic, it's more important than ever for leaders to anticipate and plan for the possibility of an unplanned event. The more prepared you are to manage shocks, the less likely you'll fall victim to the serious harm a crisis has the potential to inflict.

CM is one of several interrelated core disciplines comprising ERM, along with emergency preparedness, disaster response, BC planning, supply chain risk mitigation, and cyber liability prevention. CM practices can help lessen the magnitude of emergencies and disasters while decreasing the uncertainty and anxiety associated with these events.

Business continuity management (BCM) is a holistic management process for identifying potential impacts from threats and for developing response plans. The objective is to increase an organization's resilience to business disruptions and to minimize the impact of such disruptions. Think of BCM as the strategic process for execution when a disaster occurs. The consequence of the activation of the BC plan is a result of a disaster. In its simplest form, your organization is denied access to either/or its people, processes, or technological infrastructure.

The CM plan is often embedded into the BC plan or vice versa. This is not a problem unless the execution and responsibilities are delineated in both plans.

During a crisis, your organization is expected to execute the CM plan, and during a disaster, the BC plan. The decision-making process for the handling of the crisis or disaster is shouldered by the senior management team. The execution of the necessary crisis response and should there be a denial of access to the *people, process, and technology infrastructure,* the recovery activities under recovery strategies and BC plans will be executed.

What is confusing is the overlapping of activities for the crisis response and continuity of operations. It is good to start any discussion with the definition of a crisis and disaster. The question to ask when the incident occurs is, *Is this a crisis or a disaster?*

ERM is the process of identifying and addressing methodically the potential events that represent risks to the achievement of strategic objectives or opportunities to gain a competitive advantage.

Whereas ERM is traditionally a proactive discipline, CM is reactive. CM can be viewed as a specialized discipline within risk management, where specific practices are instituted in response to unexpected events that threaten a company's stability. Having an effective plan and resources mitigates reactivity's destructive nature.

The Board's Role in Overseeing Crisis Management

A corporate crisis can impact organizational culture, business operations, and reputation, all of which can have significant financial, legal, and regulatory ramifications. Therefore, a CM program should bring together a variety of stakeholders who can understand the potential implications and help plan for and recover from a crisis. The program should be managed by someone with in-depth legal and compliance experience who can manage day-to-day operational and tactical responses. It should also closely align the internal and external communications leaders to make sure that the decisions and messaging are clearly and directly articulated to the key audiences.

The CM program should be a process within the company's broader resiliency toolkit and integrated into its ERM program. This integration helps safeguard that crisis response planning is aligned with and informed by the company's strategic plan and risk tolerances and that it is dynamic and evolves along with changes to risk assessments and prioritization. Most importantly, a robust ERM program is foundational for risk management, litigation prevention, and loss mitigation.

CEOs and the executive team are responsible for the organization and establishment of a CM capability; boards are responsible for safeguarding the governance and viability of the organization. So, CM should be a central preoccupation for the board of every organization, small or large, local or global. Why, then, do we see so few boards actively participating in, overseeing, and assuring CM in the way they do other risks and contingency plans?

Outside of the board's responsibility for general risk oversight, the responsibility for the management of specific crises is often left unassigned. Boards should consider tasking a specific committee with the responsibility of developing a crisis response plan and running crisis response simulations from time to time. The executive or governance committees are well suited for this role and often have additional time, as compared to the audit committee, to take on this responsibility. Less frequent, but still used are special *risk committees* established by the board to specifically address the company's risk profile and develop crisis response plans. Whichever committee is selected, this group of directors should be tasked with developing and implementing each element of the crisis response plan, and most importantly that everyone involved in the crisis response plan is fully aware of the responsibility that comes with that role.

CM starts long before a crisis hits. It should be an integral part of the wider organization's resilience measures and not simply something to deploy when all other options have failed. The board should take a keen interest in the crisis capability of its executive teams. With its fiduciary duty and its responsibility to protect the interests of shareholders, this sits squarely within the board's mandate to oversee good governance and management of risk. It should be one part of the board's normal assessment of the ongoing viability and sustainability of its business (Deloitte Insights 2020).

Today's crisis response needs to be sure-footed and well-practiced to win in this environment. The board needs to know its role in advance, not learn about it upon first contact.

Our interconnected world brings increasing complexity and dependency, with global supply chains vulnerable to disruption by international events—natural and man-made. Technology has altered the balance of risk between organizations and individuals. Lone individuals with the power of technology and social media, for example, can wreak havoc across an organization.

It is this complexity that makes it increasingly difficult to make sense of the core issues at play and the trade-offs that need to be made. Today's crisis response demands more frequent moves from business as usual to a CM mode of working. The board needs to understand why, when, and how the organization moves to crisis response and to be reassured that the response is effective.

Further details on the Board's role in navigating crises are elaborated in Chapter 4.

The COBRA Model

When a board takes risk preparedness seriously, it lessens the likelihood that it will be summoned to manage a crisis. No preventative system, however, is perfect. Organizations may wish to adopt a variation of the crisis response system used in the United Kingdom at the board level.

The United Kingdom and other Commonwealth countries use a strategic, tactical, operational management structure to manage incidents. Each incident response is allocated one strategic commander on the team, one tactical commander, and as many operational commanders (geographic or thematic) as necessary to fulfill responsibilities. Thus, the strategic members function as the senior management of the response. On the political side are senior elected officials and policy makers, often referred to as the COBRA group because they meet in the Cabinet Officer Briefing Room A, located in Whitehall near 10 Downing Street, the rough equivalent of the Situation Room at the White House. A designated senior, the nonelected civil servant on each side in a formal liaison role, serves to foster an orderly flow of information between the two. This structure enables political leaders to have input into the handling of the operation while ensuring that they do not try to run it. Conversely, the strategic team members receive valuable information about the political ramifications of their decisions while remaining able to maintain an essential *battle rhythm* to keep pace with unfolding events (McNulty and Marcus 2019).

Now, translate this model to the corporate setting. Think of the corporate CM team as the equivalent of the U.K.-model strategic team and the board as the COBRA group.

Imagine a designated board liaison on the former and a counterpart member of the board on the latter (each with alternates). Assuming such roles in advance allows the CM team and the board to build familiarity, confidence, and trust. This is particularly important for the crisis manager who may have to convey hard truths to powerful board members in a vexing situation. Similarly, a board member who knows the crisis team members and how they work can provide valuable input while tempering the impulses of board members to intervene in operations.

In general, boards should not become directly involved in most crises. Responding to these is best left to senior managers who understand the details of the business. However, board members represent the shareholders and must be prepared to engage if needed. In our turbulent world, any board that is not paying attention to CM is courting disaster.

The Homefront Crisis Executive Group (HCEG)

Singapore's CM capability is the result of continual learning from past crises. The HCEG started out as the Executive Group (EG), which was set up to coordinate responses among security agencies after the Laju ferry hijack in 1974. When Hotel New World collapsed in 1986, the EG oversaw multiagency rescue efforts. Later, in 1991, the EG led security forces to resolve the hijack of Singapore Airlines Flight SQ117. When the severe acute respiratory syndrome (SARS) outbreak hit Singapore in 2003, the EG coordinated a government-wide response. SARS showed that crises are by no means restricted to security issues. They are complex with wide-ranging implications for society and the economy. Because of this, the EG was renamed and reorganized into the HCEG in 2004 (Low 2016).

The HCEG compromises senior representatives from all ministries, reporting ultimately to the elected leadership for political direction. Under the HCEG's oversight were taskforce-like Crisis Management Groups which could muster different clusters of relevant agencies to deal with different types of incidents.

While the HCEG may harness the whole public service to respond comprehensively to complex contingencies, the number of personnel to be mobilized now ranges in the thousands. At the same time, the continual drive to inculcate a whole-of-government mindset across the entire public service has helped to orient large numbers of public sector personnel—both toward improved public services and toward concerted action if a government-wide response is needed, including during times of crisis.

Designed to respond to national crises, the HCEG brings agencies across the government together to guide and coordinate a coherent whole-of-government response, factoring in an array of complex considerations.

Case Study

The HCEG's Management of COVID-19 Pandemic

While countries across the world, from the United States and Europe to the Middle East, are battling to control the rising spread of the COVID-19 outbreak, Singapore has been held up by global health experts as the model to emulate in effectively containing the global pandemic (Osterholm and Olshaker 2020).

"Singapore is leaving no stone unturned, testing every case of influenza-like illness and pneumonia," said the World Health Organization Director-General Tedros Adhanom Ghebreyesus, adding he was impressed with the government's approach "to find every case, follow up with contacts, and stop transmission" (World Health Organization 2020).

The city-state was one of the first few countries to be hit by the coronavirus contagion outside China in January 2020. But the government's swift action to impose border controls, perform contact tracing of known carriers, and use aggressive testing methods enabled Singapore to slow the rates of infection and keep the fatalities to just three so far, without overwhelming the nation's healthcare system.

This is in sharp contrast to the alarming spike in numbers in the worst-hit nations such as Italy, Iran, and the United States— where tens of thousands are infected and the mortality rate is rapidly rising. The early decisive move has also allowed Singapore to avoid sweeping school closures and business shutdowns currently imposed in most countries worldwide to blunt the accelerating pace of the virus while earning high praise.

When the COVID-19 pandemic began in early 2020, the HCEG kicked into gear—little expecting that it would be in operation for two-and-a-half years, unlike its typical activation for several intense days, weeks, or at most months.

On 22 January 2020, Singapore set up a Multi-Ministry Task Force (MTF) to manage the COVID-19 pandemic. The MTF's formation was timely: the very next day, a Wuhan tourist was confirmed as Singapore's first positive case.

The MTF's strategy was to reduce the number of cases as much as possible. This meant that contact tracing was key to reducing the risk of local community transmissions. The Ministry of Health (MOH) worked round the clock to track down and quarantine contacts with confirmed cases. As contact tracing and quarantine operations expanded, the Singapore Police Force and Singapore Armed Forces (SAF) joined MOH in the fight. The Ministry of National Development was also roped in to care for those under quarantine.

From the beginning, the MTF was transparent. It hosted daily media briefings and persisted with honest reporting of COVID-19 cases even when these numbers increased. Such transparency builds trust with citizens, and trust undergirds CM efforts. The Ministry of Communications and Information (MCI) employed differentiated media to reach specific audiences, beyond traditional print and broadcast media. Crisis response information was customized to engage senior citizens through television programs featuring popular artists, fitness workouts and e-getai (street-side variety shows featuring banter and songs) on YouTube. Programs were also developed to engage migrant workers using popular Singaporean, West Bengal, Bangladeshi, and Kollywood artists to convey important and reassuring messages through the friendsofmw.sg online portal. With the help of the Government Technology Agency (GovTech), Singaporeans were also updated with timely bite-sized information through messaging platforms such as WhatsApp and Telegram as well as a dedicated Info Bot summarizing COVID-19 information on government websites. MCI also made use of social media platforms like Facebook, Instagram, Twitter, and TikTok as well as the Digital Display Panels in public housing (HDB) lifts and lift lobbies. The Protection from Online Falsehoods and Manipulation Act provided the legal framework to quash fake news—such as a COVID-19 fatality early in the outbreak, and the closure of Woodlands MRT Station. Altogether these efforts established the Government's credibility as a trusted source of information amidst the crisis.

The calm manner in which the then Prime Minister (PM) Lee Hsien Loong addressed Singapore, and in which the MTF conducted daily press conferences, helped to steady the country's psychological posture amidst the crisis. PM Lee addressed the nation through a live TV and digital media broadcast at key junctures of the crisis, helping to frame Singaporeans' perspectives toward the situation. His speeches—along with the range of measures introduced in response to the crisis—helped to calm down a rattled population.

When a rumor circulated that Singapore was running out of face masks, the MTF assured Singaporeans that there was a sufficient supply of masks if the public were to use them sensibly and responsibly. Guided by evidence at that time, people were advised to wear masks only if unwell, to conserve masks for medical personnel. Yet, understanding public anxiety and apprehension, the MTF decided to distribute four surgical masks to each Singapore resident. Within 24 hours, SAF servicemen prepared and packed 5.2 million masks for distribution. Officers from the People's Association and citizen volunteers set up 1,000 mask collection points across Singapore. Senior citizens and vulnerable segments of society were given priority.

Ordinary Singaporeans meanwhile started ground-up initiatives to help amidst the crisis. Citizens, businesses, and nongovernment organizations donated and delivered food and essentials to families affected by the outbreak. Individual Singaporeans, companies, and community groups sent well wishes and small gifts to appreciate and cheer on frontline healthcare workers.

Recognizing the strong community response to the outbreak, the Ministry of Culture, Community and Youth developed a SGUnited portal. Under the SGUnited banner, the government rallied Singaporeans and linked volunteers with resources to generate a whole-of-nation approach toward containing the effects of the crisis.

The key thrust of Singapore's response thus far has been an institutional coordinating structure, combined with a whole-of-government mindset among public officers providing Singapore with strong CM capabilities. This readiness has allowed the government to roll out comprehensive measures aimed at protecting Singapore, with such measures delivered and calibrated with care to give priority to those most affected by this unprecedented crisis.

Conclusion

While prevention must always remain a priority, advanced crisis preparation is now imperative as avoiding crises entirely is nearly impossible. For example, the current cyber threat environment is such that it is likely only a matter of time before all businesses will suffer a cyber breach. Whether the cause of the crisis is corporate malfeasance, a terrorist attack, or a natural disaster, a company's ability to manage a timely, well-coordinated crisis response and communicate with stakeholders is critical.

CHAPTER 4

Navigating Through Crises

Board's Role

In recent years, we have seen how organizations have been tested concerning their crisis and resilience capabilities in new and various ways. A global pandemic such as COVID-19 had far-reaching implications, and many organizations also experienced ransomware attacks, major supply chain disruptions, environmental disasters, major geopolitical events, or other crises.

Boards play a key role in this crisis preparedness. A director's role is to ensure management makes the right decisions to support the long-term success and viability of an organization. Earlier identification of potential crisis events and better crisis response can have real benefits to the organization's brand and reputation, which, in turn, can translate to long-term shareholder value.

Boards will want to ensure that management is ready to handle a crisis—*before, during, and after it occurs*—whatever the crisis event might be. They can use their diverse perspectives and experiences to provide guidance and counsel to management when dealing with a crisis. After a crisis, directors will want to ensure that the organization continues to use lessons learned to improve its crisis planning. A nudge by the board to reflect on recent events and look at the effectiveness of its enterprise risk management program, crisis preparedness plan, and crisis response will benefit the entire organization. This will help the organization be better prepared when the next crisis occurs.

Organizations may be thinking that they have been through a pandemic or another crisis, so they know how to deal with one. However, performing a postcrisis review and focusing on continuous improvement will position the organization to come out ahead in the next crisis.

Before the Crisis

The best crisis plans are living documents. They are constantly updated and enhanced. It's up to the board to push management on whether the organization's crisis response and business continuity plan are up to date and ready to be deployed. This means making sure the plan has all the key elements and the right decision points. The plan should be crisis agnostic with the ability to flex to address various types of crises. It should also reflect lessons learned from what worked and didn't work in the organization's own crisis experiences. The plan can also reflect insights learned from other organizations whose crises have played out in the media. It should outline the designated crisis leader and the right cross-functional crisis team members, and it should clearly define roles and responsibilities. It should also go beyond these topics to include outside expertise needed and the communication strategy and plan. Overall, the board should have confidence that the organization can react quickly and effectively when a crisis event occurs.

The Board should understand the organization's crisis management plan. They should spend the time to do so, or perhaps management had not presented the plan or developed a crisis plan. A better plan can translate to an increased likelihood that the organization can get back to normal more quickly and minimize the operational, financial, reputational, and other effects more successfully.

Boards will want to evaluate whether the plan has considered the critical elements. They should also assess whether the plan has enough detail to ensure the crisis team knows what to do when confronted with a problem. But it's important to balance that detail with practicality. Since every crisis is different, there is no one-size-fits-all crisis plan.

It may make sense to create a crisis response team or crisis management committee, which deals with the crisis directly. Functions that should be closely involved in any crisis management activities may for example include the CEO, CFO, CRO, head of communications, head of human resources, head of IT, affected business areas, investor relations, and in-house and/or external counsel.

As boards discuss the crisis plan with management, they will want to focus on who will be the designated crisis leader or lead the crisis management committee. All eyes should not be on the CEO, who should be involved, but needs to focus his/her attention on running the business during the crisis.

The right person will have a senior leadership position and appropriate expertise, as well as stature and visibility across the business. Some organizations may identify one person to consistently lead the crisis response team; others might have a few individuals lined up to lead, depending on the nature of the crisis. Either way, the board will want to make sure the organization's plan addresses the topic.

Another critical area for boards to look at is whether the crisis plan articulates a management-level governance structure that supports effective and timely decision making, communications, and accountability. As organizations have dealt with crises, they likely experienced many competing priorities that needed immediate attention. The board will want to ensure the crisis plan articulates an approach to address this challenge with an organization-wide response. They can ask about protocols that should be put in place for different workstreams, like communications, legal and regulatory, and operations to help with decision making and working closely together during a crisis.

Boards should also ask whether the crisis plan is aligned, coordinated, and tested with the disaster recovery plan and business continuity plan. There may be other plans too, like an incident response plan if there is a cyber breach. These plans are often developed individually at an organization, but a centralized approach that includes and tests all plans together is critical for an organization's resiliency.

When a crisis occurs, the board needs to be informed at the right time. Some types of crises should trigger almost immediate notifications to the board, while in other cases, it may be appropriate to wait until the next board meeting. Recent crises that the organization has navigated can provide an opportunity for the board to reflect on and assess when it was notified, and whether that timeline was appropriate. If not, the board (working with management) can further define the board escalation expectations and the process in the crisis plan.

The Board's Crisis Plan

Beyond management's crisis plan, the board should have its plan as well. This plan will act as a layer on top of the management's plan. It should capture key elements around the board's governance structure, communication strategy, and succession planning. The plan should also capture lessons learned from the directors' experiences with corporate crises. Management should weigh in on the board's plan to ensure there is alignment of expectations. Elements these plans can include are the following:

- Preferred governance structure depending on the nature of the crisis. Will the board establish a special committee, use an existing committee, or rely on the full board? Who will serve on the special committee?
- A board communication strategy. Will there be a board liaison for the crisis team? How will board members communicate with one another? Will someone from the board need to be *camera ready*?
- Temporary succession planning. Is there a director who could step in temporarily to lead the organization, the board, or one of its committees, if necessary?

During the Crisis

Once an organization is in crisis response mode, the stakes are high. Organizations—including the board—are judged on how well they respond. And if the response is mishandled, the impact will reach far beyond an operational problem. That's when reputation and brand can be eroded.

The board has an important role during a time of crisis. It should provide the CEO and management team with guidance, support, and advice on reacting to and managing the situation. Directors' experience and expertise allow them to act as a support system and sounding board to management and to bring a different perspective to the immediacy and importance of handling a crisis appropriately.

Board members should be available to give guidance at any time and to communicate regularly with the CEO. It might be helpful to appoint a board member as a liaison to communicate with management.

Whenever necessary, external advisors, such as external legal counsel or other specialists, should be retained to advise on dealing with specific challenges.

To protect shareholder and stakeholder interests during a crisis, the board will require more frequent and current information on key risk and performance indicators. This will include a stronger focus on liquidity, cash management, risks, and stress testing.

To ensure that directors have the most relevant information, individual operational or regional managers must be aware of the type of information that is needed and at what intervals.

Directors, in turn, should be prepared to meet more often. Meetings do not have to take place in person but could and should also take the form of a video or telephone conference. Regardless of the format, directors must continue to ask pertinent questions and challenge and support management in formulating strategic responses to safeguard the organization's health.

Given that the board is usually more removed from the immediate crisis management, it can provide practical observation and alternative viewpoints on the actions taken by senior management. The board can also give feedback on proposed actions before their implementation.

Even in times when rapid response is of the utmost importance and decisions are required in the absence of full information, the board (as well as the crisis response team) should take the time to assess whether certain actions and communications are achieving the intended results or if corrective action is necessary.

There should be constant two-way communication between the CEO and chair, and the chair and the board, to ensure that all directors are informed as the situation develops. While board members will be keeping abreast of management's execution of the crisis plan and its impact on mitigating the effects of the crisis and organization performance, it is also important that directors give management sufficient space to take the actions required and embed the results without unnecessary intervention.

But as many boards and management will admit, responding to a crisis is hard. The scope of the crisis can be uncertain. Facts can be murky and inaccurate. News and rumors spread quickly through social and traditional media, adding to the pressure to respond quickly. On top of that, boards and organizations may face pressure from stakeholders, the media, and the public to act—even before they have a full picture.

As boards reflect on recent crises, they should discuss with management what went well and what didn't go well in the organization's response. A critical assessment that targets improvements and pitfalls to avoid when a future crisis occurs is valuable.

Challenge the Crisis Communications Strategy

Having the right communications strategy internally and externally is critical when responding to an event. An organization will want to tell its own story about how it is addressing the crisis. Without a communications strategy, an organization can lose control of its story, or false narratives can take hold. This can result in damage to crisis efforts and the organization's reputation. For these reasons, the board should understand and challenge management's strategy on what the organization should say, who should say it, and when they should say it.

While the board's role is usually oversight in nature, directors may be asked to communicate with certain external stakeholders in times of crisis. The board should ensure that there is always a consistent message, and that communication is accurate and proactive. External communication should form part of a larger communications framework adapted to the situation.

Importantly, people will want to know how the organization is responding, even if the answer is, *We don't know the answers yet.* Perception matters to stakeholders and acknowledging the issue is often more advantageous than staying silent.

A central aspect of any crisis response is communication—both internal and external. The employees might be worried both about their health and about job security. The shareholders and external stakeholders such as lenders will want to know what is being done and how the crisis is affecting the organization's liquidity position and its ability to continue operating. Accurate and timely information and communication are important to (re-)establish trust and to ensure the support of stakeholders.

Frequent communications and updates on the crisis are a necessity. As the crisis continues to unfold, directors should expect to get clear messaging on what is happening, who is accountable, how the organization is responding, and what will be done next to address problems in the wake of the crisis. The board should push back if the communications don't appear to align with the organization's core values, which can build significant trust with stakeholders long after the crisis is over.

Typically, the board should expect to see outside advisors built into the crisis plan and response. Law firms can advise on required communications, such as those that must be made to regulators.

They can offer perspective on how to ensure that any disclosures the organization makes voluntarily don't expose it to increased liability. Crisis communications experts can guide senior management on a communications strategy, including how frequently to make statements despite the absence of additional information.

Crisis management firms can also provide strategic advice and additional resources to help an organization balance responding to a crisis and running the business. In assessing the organization's response to recent crises, boards should ask management to reflect on whether they had all the right parties and experts involved from the start. Was there anyone that needed to be included in the last crisis that wasn't part of the plan? If so, these learnings should be updated in the crisis plan.

Boards should also be aware that while the CEO is typically the organization's main spokesperson, that can present a problem if the CEO's credibility is badly damaged—particularly if he or she is at the center of the crisis. Such cases often require someone else to step into the spokesperson role.

That may be an interim organization leader or even the board chair or lead director. The possibility of that situation means that the board should have a ready backup for the CEO in terms of a spokesperson as part of the board's crisis response plan.

It can be valuable for boards to regularly review feedback from inside and outside the organization to gauge how well the organization is responding.

Directors can follow news and social media channels to stay current, as well as get *sentiment analysis* from outside experts. Directors can also hold executive sessions with these experts just to be sure they're getting the full picture. The board will need to challenge management and demand course correction if it senses that the messages aren't working.

Management and the board should have an agreed-upon approach for board communications. The board should expect to be updated regularly on how the crisis is being handled. As boards look back on their involvement in crises, they probably had a significant increase in communications with management and board meetings. However, the board should ensure this communication is being done in the right way.

Sometimes a board designates a liaison to interact with the crisis team. Other times a board may elect to use a committee or the full board, depending on the nature of the crisis. Standing, frequent board calls can also be important. They provide an opportunity for all board members to discuss and weigh in on the latest events. These calls can occur daily or even more frequently at the height of the crisis. Whatever practices the board adopts, what's critical is that it works for the board and for the situation. By updating the board-level crisis plan with the communication preferences learned through its experiences, the board can try to create a better experience next time.

When communicating under pressure, organizations tend to focus on one or two stakeholder groups, who may have the loudest voices, at the expense of other, possibly more critical ones. Boards play a role in ensuring the communications strategy includes communications with all stakeholders and considers their diverse needs and interests. They will want to ask the crisis team for feedback from stakeholders to ensure the organization's response resonates with them and what additional actions can be taken to address concerns.

Internal communications are as important as external communications. In a crisis, management may be so externally focused that they overlook communications with their employees. Boards will want to make sure this critical stakeholder group gets attention. Employees are often the organization's strongest advocates and actively engaging with them during a crisis can help in the long term in retaining and attracting talent. Employees will continue to perform their responsibilities, deal with customers, and interact in their communities. They need to be informed about the crisis, receive regular updates, and know where to go to get more information and ask questions.

After the Crisis

Once a crisis has passed, the tendency is to get back quickly to *business as usual.* But unless there's a thoughtful postevent review and adjustments, if needed, to the crisis response plan, the organization risks repeating any mistakes it makes in future crises.

Directors will want to understand the root causes of the crisis the organization has just weathered. This allows the board to weigh in and discuss whether appropriate follow-up actions have been taken.

There may need to be an investigation based on the nature of the crisis, and management will often lead such investigations. But if management itself seems to be at the heart of the crisis, or if the event was significant enough, it may make sense for the board to decide whether an independent investigation is needed.

In addition to looking at root causes, there should be a continuous improvement mindset for the crisis response plan. Directors will want to discuss with management what was learned and how the plan will be improved as a result. It also can be valuable for management to get an external, objective assessment of the organization's crisis response from a different perspective from those who participated in it.

Once the crisis is over, a critical assessment of how well the organization responded is valuable. Boards will want to have a candid

Table 4.1 Questions for the board to consider in the postcrisis event review

Right crisis team: Did we have the right executives on the crisis team? Did we have the right internal subject matter experts, and did we leverage the right outside experts? Is the team sustainable in the event of a long-term crisis?
Useful plan: Did we have an enterprise-wide crisis response or continuity plan? Did we use it? Was it effective?
Useful plan: Did we have an enterprise-wide crisis response or continuity plan? Did we use it? Was it effective?
Clear accountability: Was it clear who had decision-making authority? Did it take too long to make decisions? Were there any bottlenecks in the process?
Effective and timely communications: Were our communications to key stakeholders on point? Were they timely and was the frequency, right? Could we have been bolder?
Stakeholder focus: Did we consider all our stakeholders? Did we address their key concerns? Were there a lot of unanswered questions?
Response to feedback: Were we agile enough to respond to feedback from our stakeholders? From the market? Did we understand what our competitors were doing and were we able to react or respond quickly, if appropriate?
Useful technology and data: Did we have the right tools to assist in our crisis response? Did we have the data we needed to make critical decisions on time? Is there a technology solution that we should have employed that would have made things easier to track crisis activities and provide relevant data and dashboards?

and open discussion with management. Table 4.1 lists the questions that boards may consider asking management.

Conclusion

To help organizations prepare for the challenge, boards should ask a series of crucial questions (see Table 4.2) to determine that the management has a practical and relevant crisis response program and actively oversee and challenge all aspects of that program, including key considerations before, during, and after an event (Klemash et al. 2018).

This includes determining that the management has the right framework in place and that it has sustainable capabilities to allow the organization to react to and quickly recover from crisis events. In preparing for and especially when confronting a crisis, boards should also understand the roles and potential implications to key stakeholders. Boards should also participate in various simulations and tabletop exercises with management teams to enhance their effectiveness in responding to crises.

It is not difficult to see how these cultural, structural, and personal fault lines can crack open in a crisis and combine to create a chasm. In essence, they all indicate insufficient trust between board members and senior managers. That may simply be frustrating in calm times but

Table 4.2 Questions for the board to consider in navigating crisis

Has the organization developed a crisis management *playbook* with decision process flows and escalation protocols? Do all the participants know their roles and the critical approval processes that are in place to be certain of quick and straightforward approvals?
Has the organization considered and challenged itself as to the types of crises it may face, where, and how likely such events might be?
Has the organization identified the individuals who will lead communications during a crisis?
Has the organization identified the external advisors in the various scenarios from whom the organization plans on seeking counsel? If so, are agreements in place with the external advisors such that they can be mobilized quickly? Does the organization have a place or virtual room secured to gather in the event of a crisis?
How often do senior leaders take part in tabletop exercises using realistic crisis scenarios? And what is the board's role in these?
Does the organization's response planning prioritize communications with key stakeholders, including employees, customers, shareholders, and business partners?
If a crisis were to unfold today, how prepared is the organization to react with precision, speed, and confidence?

escalates rapidly once a crisis starts. It is striking how often these issues came up in our conversations with directors. The point they all made, in different ways, is that a lack of transparency and trust too often hampers the effectiveness of board–management dialogue even in normal times. In a crisis, poor relationship dynamics can prove fatal.

Healthy boardroom dynamics are crucial to help an organization respond effectively in a crisis. As corporate crises are becoming more frequent and more intense, they are imposing unprecedented stresses on boards and senior management teams. In the worst cases, they can create a threat to an organization's very existence.

Board members and senior management teams need to approach preparing for a crisis much more proactively. They should go beyond the conventional crisis playbook and simulation exercises by honestly assessing how well prepared they are to manage the turbulent dynamics of a crisis. That means candidly discussing roles and responsibilities while surfacing potential vulnerabilities in organizational dynamics well before a crisis hits and preemptively agreeing on the ground rules and remedies (McKinsey 2022).

While prevention must always remain a priority, advanced crisis preparation is now imperative as avoiding crises entirely is nearly impossible. For example, the current cyber threat environment is such that it is likely only a matter of time before all businesses will suffer a cyber breach. Whether the cause of the crisis is corporate malfeasance, a terrorist attack, or a natural disaster, an organization's ability to manage a timely, well-coordinated crisis response and communicate with stakeholders is critical.

CHAPTER 5

Case Study

The "C.R.I.S.I.S." Leader in Action

A crisis is one of the greatest tests for leaders. Actions and behavior during a crisis distinguish between effective and those who are not. Effective leadership is necessary for surviving during times of crisis. Usually, crises are so unpredictable that the leader does not have time to prepare. Furthermore, no one can predict how long the crisis will last.

Effective communication between leaders and stakeholders, especially employees, is a crucial skill. Open communication on principal information, expectations, and support contributes to building trust and enables the organization to navigate in times of crisis.

It is extremely important to be honest or transparent with the employees about the magnitude of the crisis. This must always be supported with a high level of self-confidence. A crisis can create chaos in the organization due to intense emotions caused by uncertainty. Very often, when crisis strikes, the very first thing a leader must do is to seize control, stop the panic, and ensure that everyone can carry out the crisis management plan. The leader must never manifest fear because the employees need to rely on him/her every step of the way.

Leaders must be able to adapt to every situation. It is not enough to have a crisis management plan during the crisis, an effective leader needs agility to adapt and change the plan according to the circumstances.

A crisis is a situation where a leader must make hard decisions. It demands a quick response, but the decisions must be measured. The leader must quickly evaluate all the available data and decide the best way to act. This is a skill that can be developed.

Leaders must keep a positive attitude and outlook during the crisis. This does not mean that a person should be a blind optimist when the facts implicate negative outcomes. The leader creates an organizational climate that is supportive where he/she listens and empathizes with the employees. Sometimes, it is enough just to listen to the suggestions and other thoughts of team members without articulating clearly what are the expectations to navigate through the challenges during times of crisis. It is also important to always keep in mind that all crises pass sooner or later, and we should accept them and adopt disruptive mental agility with critical thinking to find optimal solutions to resolving the crisis.

Background

The organization (known as *ITS* for this case study) is a client of the Disruptive Leadership Institute LLC. ITS established over 20 years ago is an emerging player in the InfoComm technology services industry in the Association of South-East Asian Nations (ASEAN) region.

ITS clients are public sector or government agencies and government-linked companies and institutions. ITS partners with private sector firms that include developers, engineering, professional services firms, and financial institutions including banks to roll out its clients' projects.

A successful infrastructure project requires effective planning, coordination, and implementation among multiple stakeholders from start to end.

The primary role of the ITS' Project Management Office (PMO) is to establish and maintain project management standards, processes, and best practices, ensuring that projects are delivered efficiently. Furthermore, they also ensure optimal utilization of resources and help businesses achieve strategic objectives.

The PMO is responsible for aligning project management tasks with the organization's overall strategy and goals. It oversees all program and project management responsibilities across the organization and ensures that projects and programs align with its overall strategy. It is also focused on supporting project managers and their teams in successfully delivering individual projects. It provides guidance, best practices, templates, and tools to ensure consistency and efficiency in project management practices.

The PMO also facilitates clear communication channels between stakeholders and project managers to ensure alignment of goals, expectations, and activities throughout the project lifecycle. This includes regular status updates, progress reports, and meetings with key stakeholders. All of this helps in gathering feedback, addressing stakeholder concerns, and managing conflicts for successful delivery.

There are over 1,500 ITS employees across the ASEAN and the total number of employees under the PMO was 350 including the PMO Director.

The Challenge

ITS experienced a crisis, due to the CrowdStrike debacle which started on July 19, 2024. What might be considered the largest IT outage in history was triggered by a botched software update from CrowdStrike, a U.S.-based cybersecurity vendor, affecting millions of Windows systems around the world, which disrupted global business operations and upending air travel, banking transactions, and hospital care. Further details on the CrowdStrike fiasco are available in Chapter 6.

The incident disrupted significantly ITS' Windows-based information systems which regrettably impacted the project management and backend financial systems which are part of ITS' enterprise resource planning tools focused on integrating and optimizing core business processes.

The challenges this crisis posed to ITS are primarily dual-fold:

1. It impacted ITS ability in the maintenance of critical public sector infrastructure projects that it has been contracted.

2. The implementation of ongoing projects was impacted, and its ability to prioritize projects in the pipeline based on strategic goals, resource availability, and potential ROI was affected. At the same time, it affected the governance framework, including risk management, change control, and quality assurance processes, ensuring that projects are initiated, executed, and monitored following the set guidelines.

3. The CrowdStrike crisis also impacted the ITS' backend financial information systems which manage the financial payments to third-party vendors' technical consultants. These consultants were part of a project team involved in the delivery and implementation of ITS services at the client's premises. The payments to these vendors were overdue and could potentially impact ITS client's operations if these vendors halted the implementation of the projects, which are covered under the Master Services Agreement (MSA) between ITS and its clients.

The "C.R.I.S.I.S." Leader in Action

1. ITS' *Crisis Management Committee* was reconvened with clear *Terms of Reference* (goal, the authority of the committee, objectives and outcome measures, in/out of scope, whom to involve, role/responsibilities, frequency of meetings and ways of working, etc.).

2. The PMO Director was tasked to head the Committee who immediately designed and wrote the mitigation plans. He crafted the *Crisis Management Plan* with the clear goal of minimizing damage and restoring business operations as quickly as possible, particularly with minimal impact on the project delivery at the clients' end. The plan clearly outlined the processes and protocol on what and how ITS clients and relevant stakeholders including the employees and business partners should be openly informed about the current problem and the cause of the crisis.

3. Since the onset of the crisis, the PMO Director explained promptly to the clients and the other stakeholders the implications of the possibility of not being able to fulfill the obligations and complete the project requirements as part of the MSA with these clients, several of whom are public sector agencies.

4. This is critical since most of the ongoing projects are large-scale infrastructure projects with tight deadlines where any delays would impact the quality of services rendered to the public. Such delays can cause a multitude of issues, including cost overruns, damage to reputation, and the need for reworked timelines. Even a single day's delay can lead to additional costs that were not originally part of the budget.

5. The PMO Director also communicated transparently with the third-party vendors about the situation and explained the reasons that led to ITS inability to process payment of the outstanding professional fees due to these vendors. The relevant parties and stakeholders were informed that all the financial operations would be delayed until the IT outage caused by CrowdStrike was resolved and the backend financial systems were operational fully.

6. He further articulated the potential risks of penalties being imposed by the clients if any of the ongoing projects are delayed due to the inability of the project teams to complete them on schedule. Such poor track records apart from losing these clients would hurt securing future new public sector infrastructure projects and securing authorizations from relevant regulatory authorities.

7. The PMO Director also similarly briefed his team on the crisis and the potential negative impact on ITS reputation, revenue, and long-term business sustainability. He also urged all employees to maintain open and trust-based communication with the clients and all stakeholders.

8. According to the *Crisis Communication Plan*, the PMO informed the business partners (including third-party vendor consultants) about ITS' inability to pay its debt obligation due to the debacle. In certain instances, ITS offered debt payment through cession agreements as a possible solution and maintained communication with these parties during the crisis. A cession is a legal act of transfer. It encompasses an agreement that provides that the transferor or cedent transfers a right to the transferee or cessionary. The principle is that the holder/creditor of a right can cede his or her claim to his or her creditor to secure the debt that he or she owes.

Outcomes

1. The PMO Director's actions have been transparent, empathetic, and consistent communication. He was forthright about challenges, empathized with those affected, and maintained consistency in their messaging to build trust.

2. The PMO Director demonstrated effective critical thinking during the various discussions with the Crisis Management Committee. The cession agreement was a result of one of the solutions from these discussion sessions led by the PMO Director at the beginning of the crisis.

3. ITS and the PMO succeeded in maintaining relationships with the relevant stakeholders which is the result of the effective strategic and trust-based partnerships forged with these parties over the years.

4. Several of the clients generally did not immediately agree with the proposed cession agreements as proposed by ITS, but they eventually arrived at a mutually acceptable game plan while resolving the payment crisis with the third-party vendors.

5. All the ongoing project implementation activities by the third-party vendor consultants were carried out as 70 percent of them accepted the cession agreements, while the remaining (all of whom are Small and Medium Enterprises (SMEs) due to limited resource constraints and citing *cash flow* issues) decided to wait for payment before new projects were carried out.

6. During the entire crisis, the PMO Director managed to keep a positive attitude and outlook, encouraging the employees to see the crisis as an *opportunity* and lessons to be learned in strengthening ITS crisis management and business continuity planning strategy.

7. There were no employee resignations during the crisis and the PMO Director attributed this primarily to the employees' perseverance and courage to face the problems and try to find solutions.

8. The crisis did not impact revenue adversely in terms of the cancellation of new projects in the pipeline. However, the crisis did hurt slightly ITS' reputation with a few of its current clients as several ongoing projects were delayed due to the inability of a few of the third-party SME vendors to continue with the project implementation. The PMO Director immediately embarked on a *reputation recovery* mission with the challenge to rebuild relations with those impacted clients and regain their confidence. He succeeded in accomplishing that mission with his customer-centric approach that is based on empathetic listening, relationship management, and trust-based partnership.

Conclusion

One of the most important hallmarks of leading in times of crisis is controlling what appears to be uncontrollable.

The essential leadership skills during a crisis are open and transparent communication, honesty, adaptability, capability to coordinate with team members, empathy, and seeking and finding possible solutions through cognitive readiness skills including critical thinking. Through the effective demonstration of these abilities, the PMO Director as an effective crisis leader shows his team members a vision of the future, which will enable the organization to effectively function and even progress in times of crisis.

Every crisis can be handled if the leader confronts the problem and takes ownership responsibility, ensures his/her team that problems can and will be solved, and implements the day-to-day or operational activities according to the crisis management plan.

Each leader must always find a way to bring triumph to the team. Each organization is different, and each crisis has unique characteristics, but all good leaders have one thing in common: they persevere and never give up. If they fail, they do not allow themselves to be discouraged, on the contrary, they stand up and move forward. Great leaders are different from other people—they glow during difficult times such as in crisis.

An authentic leader always bears in mind that a great percentage of employees do not leave the company—they leave their managers. Leadership skills can and should be developed through continuous learning including leadership development training and executive coaching, but one must always remember that authentic leadership comes from the heart.

CHAPTER 6

Case Study

The CrowdStrike Global Crisis

On July 19, 2024, a security update issued by a U.S. cybersecurity firm CrowdStrike caused an IT outage, disrupting global business operations and upending air travel, banking transactions, and hospital care. The outage was caused by a bug in CrowdStrike's quality-control system. While initial fears of a major cyberattack proved to be unfounded, the event's impact was significant, demonstrating potential vulnerabilities in organizations' operational and cyber resilience.

The outage was the kind of crisis event that many chief information officers (CIOs) and their IT staff train for but hope never happens. The incident brought down an estimated 8.5 million Windows devices around the globe, paralyzing operations at hospitals, airlines, 911 call centers, and more (Menn and Gregg 2024). Insurers estimate the outage cost companies more than one billion dollars in revenue, with Fortune 500 companies potentially losing more than $5.4 billion (Snider 2024).

There are several lessons that we could learn from the CrowdStrike outage crisis. It is essential to emphasize the failures and the beneficial acts during any significant crisis. Even though their worldwide IT outage was a big obstacle, CrowdStrike showed several admirable activities. Here are some things they got right:

1. **Swift acknowledgment and transparency**

1. **Swift acknowledgment and transparency**
   a. George Kurtz, the CEO of CrowdStrike, publicly acknowledged the problem right away. By utilizing social media and additional communication routes, he ensured that all relevant parties were kept up to date.
   b. Kurtz managed the story and avoided disinformation with his straightforward and understandable communication. His openness in disclosing that the problem was a technical glitch rather than a security compromise was essential to keeping his clients' faith.
   c. Press releases and social media were only two of the many channels that demonstrated CrowdStrike's dedication to keeping the clients apprised of its efforts in finding a quick solution.

2. **Deployment of a quick fix**
   a. The technical team at CrowdStrike moved quickly to locate and isolate the *Falcon Sensor* software flaw. The quick response of the impacted systems in creating and implementing a remedy reduced downtime.
   b. Their ability to act quickly demonstrated their technological prowess and readiness for such tasks since it prevented additional damage and restored functionality.

3. **Customer support and communication**
   a. CrowdStrike kept lines of contact open and active with its clients throughout the crisis. Their consistent provision of updates and assistance reassured clients and upheld their trust.
   b. CrowdStrike's dedication to customer service was exhibited by open communication regarding the actions being taken and anticipated timeframes for resolution.
   c. CrowdStrike demonstrated its strengths in crisis management (CM) with its quick acknowledgment, quick repair deployment, and constant customer communication. By taking these steps, the company not only lessened the impact

of the outage but also demonstrated its dependability and commitment to its clients.

Lessons for Businesses

What to Do After the Crisis Hit

In response to the CrowdStrike outage, businesses should review their CM strategy and business sustainability plans, with a focus on building sustained cyber resilience. Doing so will help businesses identify, assess, mitigate, and transfer cyber risk and be better prepared to recover should an attack occur.

CIOs and chief information security officers (CISOs) should look to proactively incorporate new lessons in their incident response, disaster recovery, crisis communications, and contingency workforce playbooks—and revisit agreements with software providers.

Tech leaders (including CIOs and CISOs) in each organization should embark on the following immediately when such a crisis hits (Forrester 2024):

1. **Empower authorized system administrators to fix the problems quickly and effectively.**
   a. This includes backing up hard disk encryption keys as these may be critical for recovery in such instances, as well as using privileged identity management solutions for break-glass emergencies.
2. **Communicate effectively and clearly.**
   a. Communicate, both internally and externally, on the impacts, status, and progress of the organization's remediation efforts. Enlist marketing and PR to craft that messaging. Stay grounded in the realistic impacts (not the theoretical worst-case scenario) and keep an even tone.
3. **Be prepared for other unexpected events.**
   a. Crisis events require an *all hands-on deck* response but be sure to reserve a few analysts to continue monitoring other systems. Threat actors may use this time to attack while you're distracted.

4. **Pay attention to the vendor's communication strategies and follow official advice.**
   a. Follow official channels for instructions on addressing issues. Be mindful of following social media advice, especially in the age of *fake news* where incorrect or false information may result in inconsistent, conflicting, or outright incorrect/damaging advice.
5. **Put people first over process and technology (*PPT* mantra).**
   a. This disruption hit on a Friday evening in some geographies, right as people were headed home for their weekend, but tech incidents like this need support from many employees, and the teams will be working 24/7 over the weekend to recover. Organizations need to support them by ensuring that they have adequate support and rest breaks to avoid burnout and mistakes. Communicate roles, responsibilities, and expectations.

What to Do After the Crisis Subsides

Tech leaders should take the following steps once the immediate issue is fixed:

1. **Implement infrastructure automation.**
   - Infrastructure automation is a must-have for controlled and managed software rollouts. While an automated recovery is not possible in this specific instance, tech leaders should use infrastructure automation where possible to avoid manual recovery procedures, along with developing rollback and regression capabilities, and testing them often to ensure that the organization can recover to a prior state.
2. **Refresh and rehearse the organization's IT outage response plan.**
   - Regular practice of major outage response plans is vital, as is the requirement to put into practice what the team learns. Tech leaders should develop the IT outage response plan and build contingencies and communications protocols

for all major systems, services, and applications, as well as all associated recovery procedures for working with and restoring them. Create and practice a *back-out* procedure specifically for updates that don't go as planned to return to a known, good state.

3. **Get unified, written warranties from security vendors on their quality assurance processes, as well as threat detection effectiveness.**

   • CrowdStrike offers a warranty if its client suffers a breach while using its Falcon Complete platform, but this is specific to security breaches. Organizations need to ask for business interruption indemnification clauses from their vendors in the event of a software update going awry such as the current CrowdStrike one. For software that runs in trusted spaces with automatic updates, especially those that impact/use kernel modules or otherwise may impact operating system stability, this could be seen as a necessary step toward building back trust.

What CIOs and CISOs Should Do in the Longer Term

Both business and tech leaders should take the following longer-term steps:

1. **Put crisis management and incident response plans to the test.**

   a. Having a well-prepared and defined CM and incident response plan is crucial for mitigating the impacts of IT disruptions and cyberattacks. However, the truest measure of plan effectiveness is how it performs when tested in real-world scenarios.

   b. The CrowdStrike outage provided businesses with an opportunity to evaluate the efficacy of their CM plan and consider what improvements can be made. A key factor of an incident response plan is knowing when it should be activated. In this case, the outage demonstrated the need for clear activation thresholds that are understood by high-level decision makers in the organization, who are then able to assess the situation and trigger the plan appropriately. This is essential for minimizing business impact and maintaining operations.

2. **Treat the incident as a learning experience.**

   a. Although not a cybersecurity incident, business and tech leaders should view the CrowdStrike outage as comparable to one. Businesses should look back, not just at this instance but also at other security outages, ransomware, and recovery. Treat it as an opportunity to practice and say, "How would we perform if this big issue came and be able to deal with it in the future?" That way, you're not figuring it out as you go along.

   b. Moreover, experts say this kind of software error will almost certainly occur again. We should expect it to happen again, and businesses need to protect against it. There are humans involved in the entire chain of development, so invariably, there's always room for error.

c. The ongoing huge industry consolidation with fewer and fewer vendors will mean that more and more people will be affected when the next big software error occurs. Security workforces that are stretched thin will only worsen the industry's ability to respond next time. Hence, it is important to ensure that such workforces are continuously engaged so that the productivity level is optimal.

3. **Crisis communication and boots on the ground are critical.**

   a. CISOs should also re-examine their crisis communications plans, particularly internal communications. Crisis communications is essential; however, from consulting engagements in CM at the Disruptive Leadership Institute (DLI), it has been found that there are so many companies that this happened to, and they couldn't even talk to their employees. If businesses do not have a crisis communication platform, it is high time to start looking for one to make sure you can reach their employees in alternate channels when such a crisis hits.

   b. Having enough boots on the ground is also important to help with remediation. At the start of the CrowdStrike outage, both CrowdStrike and Microsoft advised organizations to manually remove the faulty update, machine by machine, an impossible task for some organizations with tens of thousands of computers. Microsoft ultimately released a program to remove the faulty updates in an automated fashion.

   c. It is crucial that all the preparation and planning of the communication strategy, for such incidents. Businesses need to have adequate people on the ground to help with their systems. There's this trend of going outsourced and making everything a Google service. But it's hard to recover from these incidents when organizations don't have anyone on the ground. As part of their business continuity or sustainability planning, businesses must keep a backup force for this, at least some minimal one, to do it.

4. **Re-evaluate third-party risk strategy and approach.**
   a. If a third-party risk management program is overly focused
      on compliance, you'll likely miss significant events like this
      one that impact even compliant vendors. Tech leaders can't
      afford to overlook assessing the vendor against multiple
      risk domains such as business continuity and operational
      resilience, not just cybersecurity. Tech leaders also need
      to map their third-party ecosystem to identify significant
      concentration risks among vendors, especially those that
      support critical systems or processes.

5. **Use the contract as a risk mitigation tool.**
   a. Tech leaders along with procurement and legal teams should
      update language to include new security and risk clauses that
      assign accountability during disruptive events and clearly
      outline timeframes for vendors to patch and remediate.
      Consider using such incidents and their impacts as a basis
      for implementing measures in contracts or service-level
      agreements (SLAs).
   b. The wave of outages involved two of the most highly
      trusted software companies, CrowdStrike and Microsoft,
      meaning CISOs can't automatically rely on software provider
      reputation to avoid disasters. Even if their names bring the
      utmost confidence to us, we should trust but verify because
      it is a human aspect, and humans make mistakes.
   c. Businesses should hold their vendors accountable for service
      level agreements, or they haven't thought about that, or
      they don't know what they are. Maturing the vendor risk
      management program is critical.

It is also crucial to work with the board and C-suite executives to
educate them on any changes needed to vendor risk management. Every
CEO and board should be asking if they have a vendor accountability
process in place with SLAs for what happens in times of crisis.

Conclusion

The initial response to any crisis sets the tone for stakeholder perceptions moving forward. In the case of CrowdStrike, effective and prompt action including transparent communications has contributed to the removal of much of the potential uncertainty and distrust among clients and investors. Leadership must ensure transparent and timely communication, both internally and externally. Our research at the Centre for Executive Education and the DLI has shown that leaders who communicate with authenticity and transparency can maintain trust even amidst turmoil and times of crisis. This involves openly sharing what is known, what isn't, and the steps being taken to address the issue.

During a crisis, how leaders treat their teams and stakeholders reflects on their leadership ethos. Leading with empathy and taking responsibility for failures help maintain morale and confidence among team members, customers, and partners. Acknowledging mistakes and taking decisive action to rectify them demonstrate a commitment to ethical leadership and corporate responsibility.

Speed is of the essence when it comes to CM. The faster an organization can respond to a crisis, the less damage it is likely to incur. Leaders should train and prepare their teams for quick actions through regular drills and by establishing clear crisis response protocols.

These leadership lessons from the CrowdStrike fiasco serve as a guide for leaders to manage crises more effectively. By embracing transparency, proactive risk management, rapid response, continuous learning, and demonstrating empathetic leadership, leaders can navigate their organizations through challenging times with integrity and resilience.

CHAPTER 7

Coaching of "C.R.I.S.I.S." Leaders

What does it mean to be an effective "C.R.I.S.I.S." leader? Leadership encircles the capability of an individual, group, or organization to guide others (individuals, teams, or whole organizations). Effective leadership requires traits that attract, impact, and influence other people (followers), the constant development of relationships with team members and other key stakeholders, professional knowledge and skills, experience, self-confidence, intuition, and empathy. Effective leaders demonstrate a repertoire of leadership styles and continuously empower their team members. Leadership skills are continuously learned and improved not only during professional development but throughout a person's life. Crises are inevitable events that occur sooner or later in all organizations. They can be triggered by different internal or external factors. Each crisis is specific and unique and requires different approaches to finding solutions to resolve them. When a crisis occurs, ignoring or avoiding it is one of the biggest mistakes for the organization. It should be accepted, resolved, and used to initiate change, which is necessary for organizations' survival and further development and growth. Having an organized, planned, and structured approach to crisis management can help minimize damage to the organization's reputation, restraining company losses and discovering inventive mechanisms to enhance employee engagement and productivity.

Crisis leadership is a process that resolves unforeseeable events that happen unexpectedly and can diminish the organizational structure, cease growth and development, and lead to catastrophic outcomes. Whether the crisis will be successfully resolved depends on how the leadership will deal with the situation. A positive approach to crisis is to accept it as an opportunity, take responsibility, manifest confidence, and implement changes that will strengthen the organization and empower the employees to perform better and become stronger people in the future. If leaders are bold and act, if they are decisive and willing to adapt their decision to the occurring conditions, they are going to have more success in resolving the crisis, compared to leaders who choose to wait and not take any action. Leadership is always a vital process, but when a crisis strikes, a strong leader is of cardinal importance for the organization.

Leadership can also be viewed as the capacity of an individual or a group of individuals to guide the members of a group or an organization. One of the crucial characteristics that every effective leader must possess is the power of influence. It is not enough only to obtain the leader title in an organization, because the person's position has nothing to do with their capability to be an effective leader. Each time the effective leader speaks, other people listen and pay attention, and he/she is the one everyone expects an answer from, for every question asked. If one cannot influence other people, they will not follow him/her.

Intuition is a distinction between extraordinary and good leaders. Extraordinary leaders instinctively know how to maintain leadership in different situations and crises, and intuitively determine if the goals are achievable with the available resources. Some people are gifted with intuition during birth, while others can develop it through training.

Trust is the bedrock of leadership. Capability, liaison, and character are the three attributes a leader must have, to earn the team's trust. Every leader must be aware that when choosing that position, he/she must stop thinking about himself/herself, so in practice, having a good character prevails over the other two characteristics, because one gains people's trust if one behaves in an altruistic manner—by putting what is best for his/her team and the organization first, before himself/herself. People need to feel secure and know they can count on their leader at any moment. Trust creates respect—people will follow one person if they respect him/her.

Great leaders know that emotion is a force that motivates people to act. Emotional connections are built and developed through personal (face-to-face) and group interactions. One must always bear in mind that one must connect to each person individually because every individual is different and unique. A leader's responsibility is to initiate and maintain these connections as a foundation of exceptional communication, loyalty, and work ethic, which is necessary for the organization's success. A strong leader encourages his/her team members to develop their knowledge and skills because he/she has faith in them. This kind of empowerment brings change, but confident people know that they can always adapt to new circumstances. Therefore, a confident leader is not afraid of this process, because the more power he/she gives, the more he/she receives.

Each leader must implement changes in the organization and find the perfect timing to do so. Change should start with small steps, through preparation and motivation. Team members should obtain the necessary skills and be motivated to want to make a change. These two steps initiate and accelerate the change implementation.

The development of leadership skills is a continuous process that requires constant learning. Our ongoing research at the Centre for Executive Education (CEE) and the Disruptive Leadership Institute unveiled that the best leaders are lifelong learners; they take measures to create organizations that foster and inspire learning throughout. Through formal education, people obtain vocational knowledge and skills, but we learn the best lessons from our daily life experiences from our failures in order not to repeat the same mistakes, and from other people with whom we interact in our personal and professional life. One must always be aware that he/she can learn from everyone and everything.

The Results-Based Leadership (RBL) Framework

There is currently extensive published research on the direct link between leadership effectiveness and sustained organizational performance. Hence, the development of the crisis leader's capability should be of primary concern for all organizations operating in a VUCAD-driven environment, since the contribution and motivation of the employees are key to achieving the organizational goals and objectives during times of crises.

Effective leaders must focus on effectively engaging all stakeholders, particularly the employees, in delivering sustainable results for their organization. In the era of the crisis-laden and disruptive-driven workplace and at a time of continued significant transition and challenge, leaders at all levels will have a responsibility to ensure that the organization's mission and purpose are at the heart of what they do.

The concept of *engagement* can be defined in many ways. Essentially, engagement is a measure of how an organization values its employees and how employees value their organization and recognize that every individual is at liberty to decide whether to do the minimum required of them or to do more (Bawany 2019). Engagement can also be taken to represent the degree of empowerment to which staff are involved in decision making and/or the openness and perceived effectiveness of communication. Hence, leaders at all levels have a key role in cultivating a strong culture of engagement. This, in essence, is the foundation of the RBL framework (see Figure 7.1), which has been effectively applied to organizations facing crises.

Step 1: Demonstrating Crisis and Disruptive Leadership Competencies

The basic premise of the RBL framework is that a highly effective transformational crisis leader would start with a strong sense of self-leadership developing a high level of self-awareness of his or her strengths and area of development in the crucial competencies for the "C.R.I.S.I.S." leader as discussed earlier. These include, but are not necessarily limited to, agility, adaptability, emotional resilience, social

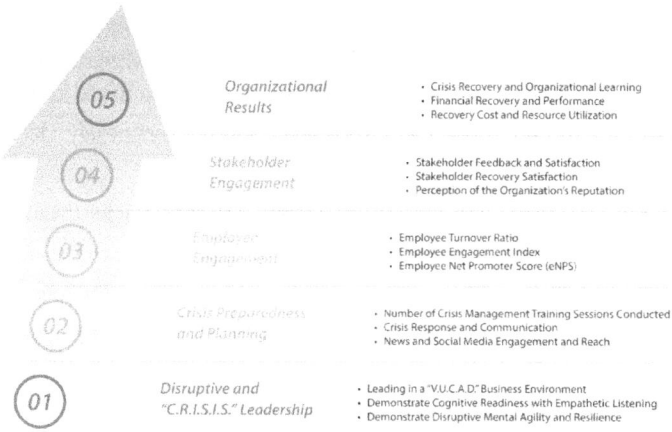

Figure 7.1 The "results-based leadership" (RBL) framework

skills, empathy, cognitive readiness, critical thinking, driving for results, innovativeness, and resilience. Next, he or she needs to lead and engage the team by being an effective managerial coach and transforming the team successfully.

Step 2: Crisis Preparedness and Planning

Key performance indicators (KPIs) are quantifiable metrics or measurements used to assess the performance and progress of an organization, team, or specific objectives. KPIs provide a way to track and evaluate key factors that contribute to the success of a business or project.

In a crisis management context, these KPIs can include metrics related to training effectiveness, response time, stakeholder satisfaction, information accuracy, recovery time, postcrisis evaluation, and implementation of lessons learned, among others.

The KPI on the total count of crisis management training sessions conducted within a specific timeframe indicates the organization's commitment to preparedness and the frequency of training activities. Tracking this KPI helps assess the extent to which the organization invests in equipping employees with crisis management knowledge and skills.

The KPI on *Time to activate the crisis management team* measures the duration between the identification of a crisis and the activation of the designated crisis management team. It reflects the organization's readiness and efficiency in mobilizing the necessary personnel to respond to a crisis promptly. A shorter time to activate the team indicates a swift and effective response, allowing for timely decision making and coordinated actions.

The KPI on *Crisis management team response time* tracks the time it takes for the crisis management team to assemble, assess the situation, and start implementing response strategies. It measures the speed and agility of the team in initiating the necessary actions to mitigate the crisis. A shorter response time demonstrates the team's preparedness, coordination, and ability to swiftly address the crisis.

The KPI on *Social media engagement and reach* measures the level of engagement and reach of the organization's crisis-related social media content. It includes metrics such as likes, shares, comments, and the number of followers or subscribers. Monitoring social media engagement provides insights into the effectiveness of the organization's communication strategies, the reach and impact of its crisis messaging, and the level of public interest or involvement in the crisis.

Step 3: Employee Engagement

The level of employee engagement is dependent on the organizational climate. Organizational climate (sometimes known as corporate climate) simply refers to how employees feel about working in the organization. Organizational climate is the process of quantifying the culture of an organization. It is a set of properties of the work environment, perceived directly or indirectly by the employees, that is assumed to be a major force in influencing employee behavior and engagement. Employees who are engaged and motivated are instrumental in delivering the required customer service experience for the client, which will result in customer engagement and retention (Bawany 2019). Consequently, engaged employees will result in employee loyalty, which will reduce the attrition rate and the operating costs of hiring new staff.

An engaged and encouraged staff may significantly impact an organization's ability to recover from a crisis. KPIs that are concerned with employee engagement and well-being assess how effectively the company is meeting the requirements of its workers. KPI such as *Employee assistance utilization* measures how often people use the crisis-related support services that were provided. The efficiency of remote work arrangements is measured by KPIs such as *Remote work productivity*. Organizations can develop resilient and motivated staff by having an effective monitoring of these KPIs.

Step 4: Stakeholder Engagement

KPIs such as *Stakeholder feedback and satisfaction* involve collecting feedback and conducting surveys from relevant stakeholders, such as customers, employees, suppliers, and the public, to assess their satisfaction with the organization's crisis response and communication efforts. It provides valuable insights into stakeholders' perceptions, concerns, and level of confidence in the organization's ability to manage the crisis effectively.

Employees who feel fully committed to the organization for which they work take great pride in doing their job. They do more than is expected of them and go that extra mile. In so doing, engaged employees, in particular, the frontline service staff or customer-interfacing employees, will have an impact and inevitably influence the buying behaviors of the customers. The excitement of an engaged employee is contagious and cannot help but rub off on the customer, especially during times of crisis.

Stakeholder recovery satisfaction KPI measures the satisfaction levels of stakeholders, such as customers, employees, suppliers, and investors, with the organization's efforts to resolve the crisis impact. It involves collecting feedback, conducting surveys, or monitoring sentiment to gauge stakeholders' perceptions of the organization's recovery actions.

The KPI such as *Stakeholder confidence and reputation management* is also relevant as the way an organization handles a crisis can significantly impact its reputation and stakeholder relationships. Measuring crisis management performance helps in assessing the effectiveness of communication strategies, stakeholder engagement, and overall reputation management during a crisis. Positive performance indicators can help rebuild trust and maintain stakeholder confidence, while negative indicators can highlight areas that need attention to safeguard the organization's reputation.

The KPI on *Organizational perception and reputation* measures the overall perception of the organization's reputation among stakeholders during and after a crisis. It includes monitoring public sentiment, media coverage, social media discussions, and online reviews to gauge the sentiment and perception of stakeholders.

Step 5: Organizational Results

The business KPIs or metrics of success for the organization especially during the time of crisis differ for each organization. However, one of the factors driving profitability and efficiency is the level of customer engagement or loyalty, since the cost of acquisition of new customers is reduced significantly. Loyalty is a direct result of customer satisfaction. Satisfaction is largely influenced by the value of services provided to customers. Value is created by satisfied, loyal, and productive employees, especially customer-interfacing service employees. Employee satisfaction, in turn, results primarily from the internal high-quality support services and organizational policies that enable the frontline team to deliver excellent service to customers.

Managers often fail to appreciate how profoundly the organizational climate can influence financial results. It can account for nearly a third of financial performance (Goleman 2000). Organizational climate, in turn, is influenced by leadership style and the way the leader motivates direct reports, gathers and uses information, makes decisions, manages change initiatives, and handles crises (Bawany 2023).

Following are some essential crisis management KPIs that are used to gauge an organizational ability to recover from a crisis and its learning capacity from a crisis:

1. *Crisis recovery and organizational learning* KPIs include the implementation of lessons learned which measures the extent to which the organization implements the recommendations and lessons learned from postcrisis evaluations. It evaluates

the organization's ability to translate insights and findings into actionable changes in policies, procedures, training programs, and communication strategies.

2. *Continuous improvement initiatives* tracks the number and effectiveness of continuous improvement initiatives implemented as a result of postcrisis evaluations. It reflects the organization's commitment to the ongoing enhancement of its crisis management capabilities. These initiatives can include training enhancements, process refinements, technology upgrades, or communication strategy improvements.

3. *Time to restore normal operations* measures the duration it takes for the organization to fully recover and resume normal operations following a crisis. It assesses the efficiency and effectiveness of the organization's recovery efforts. A shorter time to restore normal operations indicates a swift and successful recovery, minimizing the disruption to business operations and reducing financial losses.

4. *Business continuity plan activation time* measures the time it takes to activate the organization's business continuity plan (BCP) after a crisis. It evaluates the organization's readiness and ability to implement predetermined strategies and processes to sustain critical functions and minimize the impact of the crisis on business operations. A shorter BCP activation time indicates a proactive approach to ensuring continuity and resilience during a crisis.

5. *Recovery cost and resource utilization* measures the financial cost and resource utilization required to restore normal operations after a crisis. It includes expenses related to equipment repair or replacement, additional staffing, outsourcing, and other recovery-related costs. Tracking this KPI helps assess the efficiency of resource allocation and cost management during the recovery phase.

6. *Time to resolve the crisis impact* measures the duration it takes for the organization to fully address and mitigate the impact of the crisis on various aspects, such as operations, reputation, finances,

and stakeholders. It assesses the effectiveness of the organization's response strategies in resolving the immediate crisis and its aftermath.

7. *Financial recovery and performance* assesses the organization's financial recovery and performance after a crisis. It includes indicators such as revenue growth, profit margins, cash flow, and return on investment. Tracking financial recovery metrics provides insights into the organization's ability to bounce back from the crisis and regain financial stability.

In conclusion, crisis management efforts cannot be truly optimized without the use of crisis management KPIs to measure and evaluate performance. By tracking KPIs such as training effectiveness, stakeholder satisfaction, time to activate crisis management teams, and social media sentiment analysis, organizations can assess their performance, identify gaps, and take proactive measures to enhance their crisis management capabilities. Ultimately, the successful management of a crisis hinges upon an organization's ability to monitor and adapt its strategies and actions in real time.

Leveraging of Executive Coaching for the Development of "C.R.I.S.I.S." Leaders

Today's dramatically changing work environment includes crisis-laden and highly disruptive demands that organizations continuously ensure that there is a robust leadership pipeline ready to be deployed now and in the future. Identifying, assessing, selecting, and developing future leaders is, therefore, the critical strategic objective for ensuring a sustainable, competitive organization. The business case for doing so is clear as supported by extensive published research (Bawany 2019).

Executive coaching is a concept that has moved from the world of sports to the executive suite and is designed to help senior executives manage a constantly changing business environment and refine their leadership skills (Bawany 2023). However, coaching is not limited to senior levels. Increasingly, people all over the world, at all levels, utilize executive coaches to help them achieve their full potential. The process focuses on the participant's goals, reinforces learning and change, and increases self-empowerment (Bawany 2019, 2020).

Executive coaching is one of the fastest-growing and most misunderstood professions of this decade. Coaching used to be an *executive perk* for senior executives in large companies to help them make better business decisions. Today, coaching is rapidly being recognized as one of the best strategic weapons a company can have in its arsenal.

Executive coaching focuses on developing a top executive's full potential by coaching them to think and act beyond existing limits and paradigms. Executive coaching is a highly individualized form of leadership development and support available. It is based on the understanding that to be maximally effective, executives must accurately identify their strengths and areas of development, examine the impact of their behavior on others, and regularly and intentionally reflect on their values, goals, and effectiveness (Bawany 2020).

The strength of executive coaching lies in the fact that it is almost exclusively an executive development strategy that builds leadership and management strength because it is ultimately concerned with understanding where the executive is, where it is that they want to go, and the things that they would have to do to get there. It is often lonely at the top for chief executives as they generally keep their own counsel, mainly because they find it difficult to discuss matters with colleagues and cannot or choose not to share their concerns with spouses and families. Executive coaching offers a way out of this by providing an opportunity for the executive to have an independent sounding board and strategic partner in a safe and confidential environment.

Executive coaching can be defined as a confidential, highly personal learning process, involving action learning and working in partnership, combining an executive coach's observations and capabilities with an executive's expertise (Bawany 2023). The result is that the executive achieves better and faster result-oriented outcomes. It is therefore important to create a coaching environment that is founded on trust because, in a normal working day, the executive works in a fast-paced, complex, and pressured environment and there is little time to sit back and reflect on the range of issues facing him or her (Bawany 2019).

Savvy organizations acknowledge that executive coaching is a proven effective leadership intervention tool of choice for future leaders, including high potentials, for the continuous development of their leadership skills, which is critical to organization-wide success.

A study by Manchester Inc. examined the impact of coaching on 56 companies with 100 executives (Manchester Inc. 2001). Their findings suggest that 74 percent of the sponsors and 86 percent of the partici-pants were very satisfied with the process. From the survey of respond-ents who received coaching, it was estimated that coaching resulted in an average return of 5.7 times the initial investment. Furthermore, coaching contributed to a perception of increased productivity for 53 percent of respondents and improved quality of work for 48 percent of the respondents. When asked which workgroup relationships improved because of coaching, the results indicated that 77 percent reported improvement with direct reports, 71 percent reported improvement with immediate supervisors, and 63 percent reported improvement with peers. Of those receiving coaching, 61 percent reported a significant increase in their overall level of work and job satisfaction.

Executive coaching is typically seen as an ongoing relationship with no set time frame or definitive ending point. For example, the leader may have poor communication skills and unintentionally undermine direct reports, which can lead to a loss of morale and retention issues. In corrective situations, the executive coach begins by completing a full diagnosis of the situation, through the identification of undesirable behaviors, such as berating or blaming others, and will then demonstrate the consequences these behaviors will have on the individual and the organization. The coach then helps the executive identify practical ways to strengthen his leadership impact, provides direct and objective feedback, and ensures the executive gets back on track and stays on track (Bawany 2019).

Whether the relationship starts with a derailment situation or as part of a corporate-wide initiative, executive coaching covers a wide range of situations with one common goal: the personal development of a leader through the support of a professional relationship. On the organizational level, executive coaches help companies avoid costly management turnover, develop their most talented people, and ensure that leaders perform at their maximum potential. In research published in *Industrial and Commercial Training*, it was reported that executives who received coaching are more likely to be promoted or receive accelerated promotions than those who have not had one-on-one coaching (Parker-Wilkins 2006).

The ADAM Coaching Methodology

The ADAM coaching methodology (see Figure 7.2) also developed by the CEE is a structured approach to executive coaching. This consists of a four-step process that is firmly grounded in leadership development best practices.

"A" ssess

- A series of psychometric assessments and information gathering from a series of stakeholders' interviews, including the immediate manager of the disruptive leader being coached (known as the coachee), will be conducted.
- The primary objective is to determine how the coachee's performance links to current business goals.
- An assessment of the coachee's competencies, skills, styles, values, and leadership effectiveness forms the basis of the action plan.
- Gather background on the situation, identify the purpose of the coaching engagement, and discuss expected outcomes.

The ADAM Coaching Model for Developing "C.R.I.S.I.S." Leaders

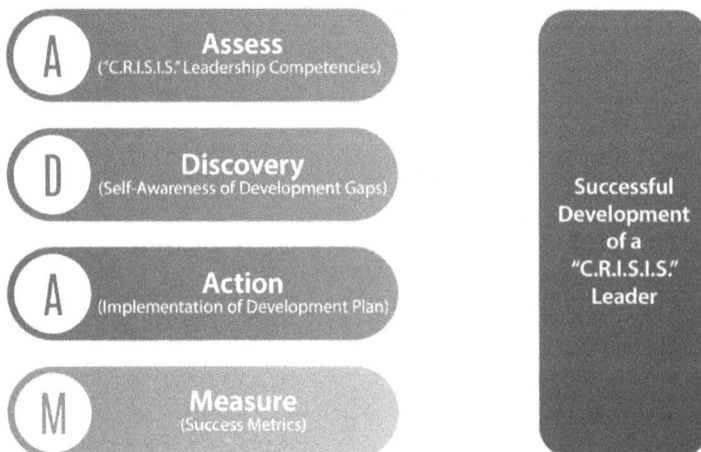

A	**Assess** ("C.R.I.S.I.S." Leadership Competencies)
D	**Discovery** (Self-Awareness of Development Gaps)
A	**Action** (Implementation of Development Plan)
M	**Measure** (Success Metrics)

Successful Development of a "C.R.I.S.I.S." Leader

Figure 7.2 The ADAM coaching methodology

- Conduct an in-depth coachee interview, including life and career history, self-perceived behavioral and leadership strengths and shortcomings, and desire to close the gap on weaknesses and further develop the strengths.
- Hold a tripartite session with coachee and sponsor (the coachee's immediate manager), to obtain the senior management's commitment, and define the degree of confidentiality.
- Provide an overview of the coaching process, timetable, and parameters of the engagement.

"D" iscovery

- Meetings are scheduled to review the assessment data.
- The coachee will be provided with feedback based on the results of the assessments that have been undertaken.
- Development objectives are discussed between the coachee and the coach to link the feedback received with the agreed business goals and professional objectives.
- Based on the key objectives identified, coaching activities and timelines are developed jointly between the coachee and the coach.
- The coachee, with the support of the coach, will develop an action plan that will enable coachees to determine what to do to close the gaps in their leadership capability.
- The coach and the coachee form a working alliance where the coach provides the stimulus and environment for the coachee who will write the action plan.
- The plan is formalized and shared by the coachee with the sponsor for agreement and support of the action plan and expected development outcomes.
- The sponsor will sign off on the development plan to ensure that there is alignment with the business objectives.

"A" ction plan

- The coachee will implement the development plan by taking well-defined action steps and regular feedback during scheduled monthly coaching sessions with the coach, which enables the coachee to move toward measurable goals.
- *Shadowing* or observation of the coachee at work (as needed and if appropriate).
- Specific actions are taken to develop the key skills and knowledge agreed to in the development plan. These actions may include:
  - Behavior modification and efforts to use new behaviors.
  - Building new skills and competencies while refining others.
  - Developing key relationships within the sponsoring organization.
  - Communication strategies for successful networking and being an ambassador for the sponsoring organization.
  - The sponsor and coach communicate, in person, by phone, or through email, to discuss specific situations and maintain focus on the objectives of the development plan.
  - There is also an opportunity for contact with the sponsor to monitor progress, as defined within the parameters of the sponsoring organization's/coach confidentiality agreement.

"M" easure

- A full evaluation of the coaching process and engagement based on the agreed success metrics at the beginning of the assignment yields objective measures of business results and professional outcomes for both the organization and the coachee.
- Periodically, and after the coaching program, the coachee and the coach will discuss progress against the plan and determine action plans as appropriate.
- A final tripartite coaching meeting will be held, where the results of the coaching engagement will be presented to the sponsor.

- The recommended next step for the continuous professional development of the coachee will be discussed and agreed upon with the sponsor.
- The consistent ADAM coaching delivery methodology ensures that every coachee receives the same degree of insightful business analysis, personalized consideration, and performance-driven priority.

Case Study on Developing a "C.R.I.S.I.S." Leader

The following case study illustrates how executive coaching as an intervention has been successfully applied in the development of a leader who has been identified through the Assessment & Development Centre to be a "C.R.I.S.I.S." ready leader.

The Situation: Ensuring a "C.R.I.S.I.S." Ready Leader at the Workplace

The said manager, belonging to Generation X (born between 1964 and 1979), has been with the organization for over 30 years. He was promoted to the role of senior vice president of operations and technology at a global bank. The manager has a solid record of success in his previous roles where a hands-on, controlling style with staff direct reports was an effective managerial tool. However, in his new position, he faced broad operational responsibilities and managed multiple stakeholders both internally and externally. The manager needed to lead cross-functionally by bringing together departments throughout the organization including strategy, finance, marketing, distribution, IT, and technical operations. The makeup of most of the employees from these various functions is those of his generation and that of Generation Y (born between 1980 and 1994).

With significantly more Gen Years under his leadership, the manager's communication style was soon found to be confrontational and abrasive and often prevented him from building trusting relationships with key stakeholders. His style also jeopardized negotiations with existing and potential key business alliances, channels of distribution, and vendors.

Several of the senior leadership team members including the chief information officer, chief data officer, and chief technology officer perceived that the manager was perhaps unwilling or unable to adapt to the intended role as a *crisis-ready* leader. It was soon apparent that if left unchecked, the situation could impact not only the manager's credibility but most importantly the corporation's strategic objectives during times of crisis should he be tasked to lead the crisis management strategy of the organization. Not counting the loss of productivity, the loss of crucial talent, and their replacement costs alone are expected to be substantial.

The chief human resources officer (CHRO) recommended to the CEO that an external professional executive coach would be a useful resource for addressing the managerial challenges faced by this manager. The CEO, who is a strong advocate for leadership development, believed that the manager, whom he has known over the years, can be developed. Hence, upon reviewing the business case put up by the CHRO and the human resource business partner, the CEO agreed to the engagement of an executive coach.

Coaching Strategy: Assessment, Feedback, and Development of New Behavioral Skills

During the first stage of the coaching process, the manager (*coachee*) completed a group of assessments including a 360° feedback leadership effectiveness profile (based on the "C.R.I.S.I.S" leadership framework) to provide objective information about his communication and leadership styles. Feedback from project team members, peers, and direct reports, combined with a series of constructive conversations with the key senior management team including the CEO and CHRO, provided a clear insight into the style, competencies, and behaviors that are expected from the role of a crisis leader. This data enabled the coachee to see the impact his behavior had on others and how it could impact his success in building relationships and reaching business outcomes.

A developmental plan was written by the coachee and reviewed with his executive coach to address gaps in areas of communication, collaboration, relationship management (social skills), empathy, critical thinking, and conflict management. More effective techniques and approaches were role-played with the coach, and the coachee was encouraged to use these new behaviors by leveraging the best practice tools, framework, and approaches introduced by the coach; during the conversations that the coachee had planned weekly, individually with each team member as well as in project team meetings. The coaching goal was to increase the manager's effectiveness in all his business endeavors and to increase his ability to improve the organization's success through managing the stakeholders as well as leading and engaging his team in a much more effective manner than before.

Results: Tremendous Improvement in the Crisis Leader's Communication Style and Relationship Management Skills Observed

Feedback received by the CHRO, and the other senior leadership team members was that there is much more open and trust-based communication between the coachee and his team members as well as with the other stakeholders; key sensitive strategic alliances were successfully negotiated.

The manager was better able to communicate with and facilitate information transfer among his team of primarily Gen Years, whom over six months, he was able to transform into a high-performance team. A follow-up 360° leadership assessment was conducted where a positive change in the manager's leadership and communication style was perceived by the various stakeholders.

Due to the success of this coaching intervention, executive coaching is now being used more broadly as a tool to enhance leadership development among future crisis leaders, resulting in the achievement of both tactical and strategic objectives of the organization (Bawany 2020).

Conclusion

The development of leaders includes the process of transitioning them effectively into a crisis leadership position. This could be smoother if these leaders developed a sense of optimism and monitored and managed their outlook and perspective. Executive coaching, mentoring, action learning workplace projects, leadership masterclass training, stretch assignments, and executive education along with the relevant tools and systems are very important for the effective development of these future leaders. However, without the right outlook and unwavering support from the senior leadership team, new and even seasoned leaders will experience serious difficulties and unrest (Bawany 2019).

Crisis leaders need to reflect on and examine their leadership attitude and perspective and develop a plan to work on areas that need improvement. Executive coaching can work to bring out the best in future crisis leaders through the support of a professional relationship. The relationship must be built on a foundation of trust and confidentiality. The ability of coaches to provide leaders as an outside resource that can also act as a sounding board can help them become the successful leaders they were meant to be (Bawany 2019).

Organizations must clearly define the purpose of coaching, gauge the process, and evaluate the results. Coaching is not just about providing support. Ultimately, coaching should deliver what any business needs—real results (Bawany 2019).

CHAPTER 8

Are You Ready for the Next Crisis?

We are living in an era of constant disruptions and crises!

First, the COVID-19 pandemic: It upended lives and livelihoods as it turned our lives and economies upside down—and it is not over. The continued spread of the virus could give rise to even more contagious or worse, more lethal variants, prompting further disruptions—and further divergence between rich and poor countries.

Second, the war: Russia's invasion of Ukraine, devastating for the Ukrainian economy, is sending shockwaves throughout the globe. Above all is the human tragedy—the suffering of ordinary men, women, and children in Ukraine, among them millions of displaced people. The economic consequences from the war spread fast and far to neighbors and beyond, hitting hardest the world's most vulnerable people. According to the managing director of the International Monetary Fund (IMF), hundreds of millions of families were already struggling with lower incomes and higher energy and food prices. The war has made this much worse and threatens to further increase inequality (International Monetary Fund 2022).

She further adds that:

> for the first time in many years, inflation has become a clear and present danger for many countries around the world. This is a massive setback for global recovery. In economic terms, growth is down, and inflation is up. In human terms, people's incomes are down, and hardship is up.

These double crises—pandemic and war—and our ability to deal with them are further complicated by another growing risk:

fragmentation of the world economy into geopolitical blocs—with different trade and technology standards, payment systems, and reserve currencies.

Such a tectonic shift would incur painful adjustment costs. Supply chains, R&D, and production networks would be broken and need to be rebuilt. Poor countries and poor people will bear the brunt of these dislocations. This fragmentation of global governance is perhaps the most serious challenge to the rules-based framework that has governed international and economic relations for more than 75 years and helped deliver significant improvements in living standards across the globe (International Monetary Fund 2022b). It is already impairing our capacity to work together on the two crises we face. And it could leave us wholly unable to meet other global challenges—such as the existential threat of climate change.

The Major Future Disruptors Leading to Crises

There are possibly six megatrends of future disruptive forces (see Figure 8.1) that would lead to potential crises in the coming decades.

Climate Change

The impacts of climate change are felt across all industries. The climate crisis is changing the way we live and the way we work.

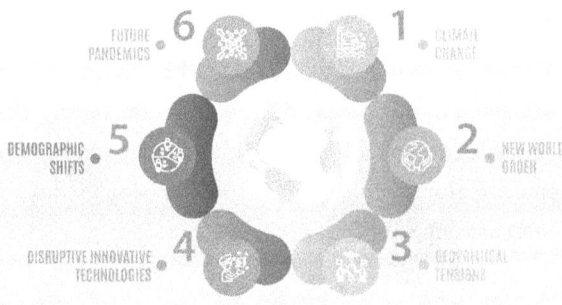

Figure 8.1. Crises resulting from mega forces disrupting the global supply chain

The effects are already being felt across many businesses in most industries. However, climate change and the transition to a net-zero future could create new industries and new growth opportunities for businesses, which will bring new jobs and revitalize economies.

But there is a downside. Almost all industries are also threatened by the effects of climate change, either directly or indirectly. For companies thinking about the ways the changing climate might affect their business, they should consider the risks that broadly fall into three categories: physical, transition, and liability risks.

The physical risks of climate change are immediate threats that come from the environment. These include flooding, hurricanes, drought, wildfires, and other natural hazards that are exacerbated by climate change and can cause physical damage to people, property, and critical infrastructure.

The agricultural sector is particularly exposed to physical climate risks. Flooding and drought can pose a risk to crops and livestock, as do extreme cold and extreme heat.

The UN climate report highlights that the threat to our planet is not going away (UN Climate Change 2022a). On the contrary, it is getting worse. We must mitigate it everywhere, adapt where necessary, and build resilience against the shocks to come.

We know what needs to be done: a comprehensive approach including carbon pricing and investment in renewables, with compensation and new opportunities for those adversely affected by the green transition. These measures can also bolster energy security (UN Climate Change 2022b).

The IMF Executive Board approved the creation of a new Resilience and Sustainability Trust. By providing affordable longer-term funding and catalyzing private investment, it will help address macro-critical challenges such as climate change—and future pandemics (International Monetary Fund 2022b).

A critical mass of the world's largest companies and countries have now made net-zero pledges, creating a snowball effect that will encourage others to join. As net zero rapidly becomes the standard for government and corporate commitments, it's appropriate to stop and ask: Is net zero a sufficient tool to address climate change? How can businesses leverage net-zero emissions strategy to offer the abatement of climate risk for shareholders without abrupt disruption to near-term returns and achieve reputational benefits for companies that serve customers or businesses that are climate-conscious? What are the significant limitations to the approach, which, if unaddressed, could easily misrepresent and undermine progress toward the ultimate goal of environmental sustainability?

The New World Order

In the world order, there is a tendency toward multipolarity, which, in turn, may imply realignment into regionally and ideologically aligned groups. This immediately raises questions of what might that multipolarity look like in practice. According to the Boston Consulting Group research, the global economy will lose up to $10 trillion in Gross Domestic Product (GDP) in 2025 unless governments repeal or reduce tariffs and nontariff barriers that currently obstruct global merchandise trade, according to a new report released today for G20 governments (Anaya et al. 2020). Will the economy remain global in nature, and will we find new workable mechanisms to cooperate beyond the economy? Moreover, years of relative moderation in international politics seem to be giving way to more political polarization between blocs. How effectively will global and local institutions and leaders adapt to, and shape, this different world order?

Geopolitical Tensions

The first geostrategic theme will be continued shifts in geopolitical power and the international system. The two-tiered world will contribute to these shifts. So too will relations among the great powers—the United States, Russia, and China—which will be somewhat inwardly focused while also competing with each other for global influence. While these great-power dynamics are creating a multipolar system, how will the variety of middle powers play a larger role in their regions and on the global stage? To what extent will the conflict between Russia and Ukraine create further severe geopolitical and economic shockwaves with lasting effects? What are the implications if the South China Sea geopolitical flashpoint evolves into a truly global conflict?

Disruptive Innovative Technologies

Across technology platforms, the key drivers of the most recent era's digitization and connectivity seem to be approaching saturation. Yet, a set of already potent transversal technologies, particularly artificial intelligence (AI) and bioengineering, may combine to create another big surge of progress in the next era.

In the next global economic downturn, AI is likely to threaten a wider range of jobs than in past cycles, including higher skilled cognitive jobs. Jobs in advanced economies are at risk of being replaced by AI. In other words, the pool of potentially replaceable workers in future downturns will be bigger than anything we've seen before. The result could be unprecedented job losses.

That could also lead to unprecedented numbers of long-term unemployed because many of the displaced workers will lack the requisite skills in an economy where AI is increasingly prevalent.

Such a sharp spike in unemployment would be a major shock to the financial system, as record numbers of unemployed workers could struggle to repay their debts. However, in this new AI-adapted reality, that would be only part of the disruption to the financial system.

Metaverse is another disruptive innovative technology. It is a collective virtual shared space, created by the convergence of virtually enhanced physical and digital reality (Wiles 2022). It is persistent, providing enhanced immersive experiences, as well as device independence and accessibility through any type of device, from tablets to head-mounted displays. The metaverse will impact every business that consumers interact with every day. According to Gartner, the metaverse is where a quarter of us will be working, studying, shopping, and socializing for at least an hour a day by 2026.

Another disruptive technology that took the world by storm in 2023 is the rise of generative AI such as ChatGPT, which has the potential to be a major game-changer for businesses. This technology, which allows for the creation of original content by learning from existing data, has the power to revolutionize industries and transform the way companies operate. By enabling the automation of many tasks that were previously done by humans, generative AI has the potential to increase efficiency and productivity, reduce costs, and open up new growth opportunities. As such, businesses that can effectively leverage technology are likely to gain a significant competitive advantage.

The other disruptive technology that would have an impact on businesses globally is artificial general intelligence (AGI). AGI possesses the capacity to comprehend, learn, and execute tasks with human cognitive abilities and engenders significant anticipation and intrigue across scientific, commercial, and societal arenas. Much has already been written about the likely impact of AI and the importance of carefully managing the transition to a more automated world. Leaders need to understand and appreciate the impact of machines achieving human-level intelligence such as AGI, indicators by which to measure progress, and actions they can take to begin preparations today (Berruti et al. 2020).

The big questions remain. What impact will this next wave of disruptive innovation technologies have on businesses, work, and social order? How are organizations ensuring their workforce readiness to leverage these latest technologies?

Demographic Shifts

In demographic forces, a young world will evolve into an aging, urban world, and inequality within countries may increasingly challenge the social fabric. The majority of the world's workforce is aging rapidly while, at the same time, we see the rise of Generation Z, also known as *digital natives*. This major demographic shift is bringing an end to the abundance of labor that has fueled economic growth since the 1970s. Thanks to longer and healthier lives, many people are working well into their 60s and beyond, but the trend toward later retirement is not likely to offset the negative effects of aging populations. As the total size of the labor force stagnates or declines in many markets, the momentum for economic growth should slow. How will governments and businesses address the major challenges, including surging healthcare costs, old-age pensions, and high debt levels? How will countries, institutions, and individuals adapt to demographic changes—will we age *gracefully*?

The Next Global Pandemic

In the wake of COVID-19, there have been calls for the world to be better prepared for the next pandemic. These calls are driven by a sense that the outbreak could have been foreseen and prevented or that the spread could have been more effectively contained, causing less social and economic disruption and averting deaths. Yet, the world tends to move on quickly, with new crises taking center stage, resulting in the now familiar cycle of *panic and neglect*. This is a concern: Although the timing and nature of the next pandemic spark are unknown, it is certain to happen. How can governments and businesses address the limitations of past efforts and the need for a more ambitious and sustained approach to preparedness? What roles do global institutions play in ensuring more financing, reform of global governance for health-related crises, and fresh thinking around global public goods?

Crisis Resulting From Supply Chain Disruption

Years of supply chain disruption and variability in customer demand have led to a feeling of permanent crisis for many organizations. This rollercoaster will stop anytime soon.

Today's supply chains are not set up to handle the new speed of delivery, customer convenience, and the blurring of channel boundaries, so their physical network design and future operating model may require major adjustments. Supply chains must *pivot or perish* in response to immediate risks and challenges.

The risk facing any industry value chain reflects its level of exposure to different types of shocks, plus the underlying vulnerabilities of a particular company or in the value chain. We, therefore, examine the growing frequency and severity of a range of shocks, assess how different value chains are exposed, and examine the factors in operations and supply chains that can magnify disruption and losses. Adjusted for the probability and frequency of disruptions, companies can expect to lose more than 40 percent of a year's profits every decade, based on a model informed by the financials of 325 companies across 13 industries (McKinsey 2020). However, a single severe shock causing a 100-day disruption could wipe out an entire year's earnings or more in some industries—and events of this magnitude can and do occur.

Trade tensions between the United States and China as well as between Russia and European companies (as a fallout of the Russian invasion of Ukraine in February 2022) and now the COVID-19 pandemic have led to speculation that companies could shift to more domestic production and sourcing. We examined the feasibility of movement based on industry economics as well as the possibility that governments might act to bolster domestic production of some goods, they deem essential or strategic from a national security or competitiveness perspective. Moving the physical footprint of production is only one of many options for building resilience, which we broadly define as the ability to resist, withstand, and recover from shocks. Technology is challenging the old assumptions that resilience can be purchased only at the cost of efficiency. The latest advances offer new solutions for running scenarios, monitoring many layers of supplier networks, accelerating response times, and even changing the economics of production. Some manufacturing companies will no doubt use these tools and devise other strategies to come out on the other side of the pandemic as more agile and innovative organizations.

To understand the full range of potential disruptions and avoid the trap of *fighting the last war*, companies must look beyond the latest disaster. Not all shocks are created equal. Some pass quickly, while others can sideline multiple industry players for weeks or even months. Business leaders often characterize shocks in terms of their source. These may include force majeure events, such as natural disasters; macropolitical shocks, such as financial crises; the work of malicious actors, such as theft; and idiosyncratic shocks, such as unplanned outages. But characteristics beyond the source of a shock determine its scope and the severity of its impact on production and global value chains.

Today, much of the discussion about resilience in advanced economies revolves around the idea of increasing domestic production. However, the interconnected nature of value chains limits the economic case for making large-scale changes in their physical location. Value chains often span thousands of interconnected companies, and their configurations reflect specialization, access to consumer markets around the world, long-standing relationships, and economies of scale.

Reshaping Your Organization's Supply Chain Resilience

Extended supply chain visibility and continuous monitoring of product flow support resilience. Understanding how products flow across the value chain, with forward-looking/sensing capabilities, is essential for organizations that depend on global/regional complex supply chains with long lead times, as well as those exposed to volatile environments.

Supply chain leaders know they need to gather data, analyze it, and use the insights to fast-track decisions and be more responsive to unplanned events and opportunities. Some companies that we surveyed have collaborated with manufacturers to track inventory and fulfillment of orders using the closest warehouse to the customer to reduce logistics costs. This developed into a service offering that provides customers and suppliers with a variety of data uses and applications. This ranges from data warehousing and smart applications with predictive capabilities to clickstream analysis for improved digital customer experiences and a better understanding of website performance.

Building organizational agility into *business-as-usual* has been a challenge for decades, and organizations are often impeded by the leaders' and managers' lack of disruptive mental agility and suite of disruptive leadership competencies. Many of them have a misguided belief that agility and resilience cannot work together. On the contrary, our research has shown that the two can be complementary.

Today's business environment demands organizations to adopt organizational learning as a source of sustainable competitive advantage. This means they need to learn to scale and deliver growth at clock speed while enabling agility and sustainability.

Enabling growth today in an era of constant disruptions and crises would require a deliberate focus on elasticity: building agility and sustainability into the design of the organization while ensuring that the business can meet strategic business objectives and goals. Companies need to adhere to evolving societal standards and operate using sustainable business practices to scale and drive growth. Opting in or opting out of sustainability is no longer an option. Sustainable organizations expand the term *performance* to optimize environmental, social, and governance outcomes as well as financial results.

Conclusion

Organizations must be ready for future disruptions which would evolve into crises if they were not well prepared. There will be other potential forces that are creating new and constant waves of disruption—creating both opportunities and risks.

Companies experiencing fast growth must build an agile and sustained organization designed to rapidly deploy and redeploy talent and resources without denigrating operational capability in other areas. Capability building includes everything from training on how to run virtual meetings and executive coaching to workshops focused on teaching fundamentals around how to lead change. While companies face a significant opportunity to expand and realize revenue and profit growth, they may not always readily have the organizational capabilities to do so effectively. Why? For one, external disruptions to a given market (e.g., new regulations, innovations, and customer performance requirements) can quickly make current business and/or operating models less viable. Organizational designs must be able to outpace disruptive changes of environmental jolts, economic shocks, and more classical reorganizations.

To evolve, organizations need to develop continuous change capabilities. For organizations seeking to scale and grow, not only should their leaders inspire change and be effective *change agents*, but they also need to adopt an integrative and future-focused approach to their strategic redesign, allowing them to integrate structure, people, process, and technology as leverage points to drive growth. Engaging leaders at all levels aligning their growth and disruptive mindsets and provid-ing the relevant incentives to reinforce new behaviors go a long way toward executing large-scale organizational design efforts and growing the company.

Research by the Centre for Executive Education and the Disruptive Leadership Institute on best-in-class organizations that have successfully navigated disruptive challenges showed that they took concrete steps to dramatically improve their capacity to mitigate the risks associated with crises by anticipating, responding to, and capitalizing on the disruptive forces heading their way.

References

Almond, G.A., S. Flanagan, and R. Mundt, eds. 1973. *Crisis, Choice, and Change: Historical Studies of Political Development.* Boston: Little Brown.

Anaya, P., N. Blyth, R. Hanspal, M. McAdoo, S. Ramachandran, K. Ramadurai, and S. Schram. September 17, 2020. *The $10 Trillion Case for Open Trade.* Boston Consulting Group.

Ardern, J. 2020. "Major Steps Taken to Protect New Zealanders From COVID-19 [Press Release]." Accessed on December 2, 2022. www.beehive.govt.nz/release/major-steps-taken-protect-new-zealanders-covid-19.

Aten, J. March 20, 2020. "Marriott's CEO Shared a Video With His Team and It's a Powerful Lesson in Leading During a Crisis." *Inc.* Accessed on December 12, 2022. www.inc.com/jason-aten/marriotts-ceo-shared-a-video-with-his-team-its-a-powerful-lesson-in-leading-during-a-crisis.html.

Bass, B.M. and R.M. Stogdill. 1990. *Bass & Stogdill's Handbook of Leadership: Theory, Research, and Managerial Applications.* New York, NY: Free Press, Collier Macmillan.

Bawany. 2015a. Results-based Leadership: Putting Your Employees First before Customer & Profits. *Leadership Excellence Essentials*, HR.com

Bawany, S. 2019. *Transforming the Next Generation of Leaders: Developing Future Leaders for a Disruptive, Digital-Driven Era of the Fourth Industrial Revolution (Industry 4.0).* New York, NY: Business Express Press (BEP) Inc. LLC, United States of America.

Bawany, S. 2020. *Leadership in Disruptive Times.* New York, NY: Business Express Press (BEP) Inc. LLC.

Bawany, S. 2023. *Leadership in Disruptive Times: Negotiating the New Balance.* New York, NY: Business Express Press (BEP) Inc. LLC.

Berruti, F, P. Nel, and R. Whiteman April 29, 2020. *An Executive Primer on Artificial General Intelligence.* McKinsey Global Institute, McKinsey & Company.

Božič, K. and V. Dimovski. 2019. "Business Intelligence and Analytics for Value Creation: The Role of Absorptive Capacity." *International Journal of Information Management* 46: 93–103. https://doi.org/10.1016/j.ijinfomgt.2018.11.020.

Chartrand, J., H. Ishikawa, and S. Flander. 2018. "Critical Thinking Means Business: Learn to Apply and Develop the #1 Workplace Skill of the 21st century!" White Paper, Pearson TalentLens.

Davenport, T.H. and J.G. Harris. 2007. *Competing on Analytics: The New Science of Winning*. Harvard Business Press.

Deloitte. 2020. *COVID-19: Managing Supply Chain Risk and Disruption*. Deloitte Development LLC. Accessed on December 21, 2022. www2.deloitte.com/ca/en/pages/finance/articles/covid-19-managing-supply-chain-risk-and-disruption.html.

Deloitte Insights. 2020. *The Journey of Resilient Leadership*. Deloitte Development LLC.

Disruptive Leadership Institute. 2022. *Crisis Leadership Lessons Learned From the Front Lines: Navigating the Disruptive Leadership Challenges of the COVID-19 Pandemic & the Fourth Industrial Revolution (Industry 4.0) at the Workplace*. Singapore: Disruptive Leadership Institute. Accessed on January 3, 2023. www.disruptiveleadership.institute/research-reports/.

Drennan, L. and A. McConnell. 2007. *Risk and Crisis Management in the Public Sector*. London: Routledge.

Dweck, C.S. 2006. *Mindset: The New Psychology of Success*. Random House.

Edmondson, C.A. March 6, 2020. "Don't Hide Bad News in Times of Crisis." *Harvard Business Review*.

Fink, S. *Crisis Management: Planning for the Inevitable*. New York. AMACOM, 1986.

Forrester 2024. CrowdStrike Global Outage. "Critical Next Steps For Tech and Security Leaders." Forrester Research, Inc. Assessed on August 12, 2024. www.forrester.com/blogs/crowdstrike-global-outage-critical-next-steps-for-tech-and-security-leaders/.

Friedman, U. April 19, 2020. "New Zealand's Prime Minister May Be the Most Effective Leader on the Planet: Jacinda Ardern's Leadership Style, Focused on Empathy, Isn't Just Resonating With Her People; It's Putting the Country on Track for Success Against the Coronavirus." Washington, DC: The Atlantic. Accessed on January 10, 2022. www.theatlantic.com/politics/archive/2020/04/jacinda-ardern-new-zealand-leadership-coronavirus/610237/.

Georgieva, K. April 14, 2022. *Facing Crisis Upon Crisis: How the World Can Respond*.

Goleman, D. March–April 2000. "Leadership That Gets Results." *Harvard Business Review*: 15–29. Harvard Business School Publishing.

Goleman, D. 2002. *Primal Leadership: Realizing the Power of Emotional Intelligence*. Boston, MA: Harvard Business School Press.

International Monetary Fund. October 11, 2022b. *World Economic Outlook* Report October 2022. International Monetary Fund (IMF). www.imf.org/en/Publications/WEO/Issues/2022/10/11/world-economic-outlook-october-2022 (accessed on October 4, 2024).

Kets de Vries, M.F. 2004. "Putting Leaders on the Couch. A Conversation With M.F.R. Kets de Vries. Interview by Diane L. Coutu." *Harvard Business Review* 82: 64–71, 113.

Klann, G. 2003. *Crisis Leadership: Using Military Lessons, Organizational Experiences, and the Power of Influence to Lessen the Impact of Chaos on the People You Lead, Center for Creative Leadership.* NC: Greensboro.

Klemash, S., J. Smith, and J. Lee. October 7, 2018. *The Board's Role in Confronting Crisis, Harvard Law School Forum on Corporate Governance.*

Lichtheim. 1973. Ancient Egyptian literature: a book of readings. Vol.1. *The Old and Middle Kingdoms.* London, Berkeley

Low, J. December 2016. "Singapore's Whole-of-Government Approach in Crisis Management." *Ethos* (16). Civil Service College Singapore.

Luecke, R. and L. Barton. 2004. *Crisis Management: Master the Skills to Prevent Disasters.* Boston, MA: Harvard Business School Press.

Mair, V.H. 2007. *Danger + Opportunity ≠ Crisis: How a Misunderstanding About Chinese Characters Has Led Many Astray.* Pinyin.info.

Manchester Inc. 2001. *Executive Coaching Yields Return on Investment of Almost Six Times Its Costs,* 2–3.

McKinsey. October 1, 2011. *The Business of Sustainability.* McKinsey Global Institute. New York, NY: McKinsey & Company.

McKinsey. March 2017. "The Digital Reinvention of an Asian Bank: The CEO of DBS Says It's Not Enough to Apply Digital 'Lipstick'." *McKinsey Quarterly,* March 2017 Issue. New York, NY: McKinsey & Company.

McKinsey. August 6, 2020. *Could Climate Become the Weak Link in Your Supply Chain?* McKinsey Global Institute. New York, NY: McKinsey & Company.

McKinsey. 2022. "The Board Perspective: A collection of McKinsey Insights Focusing on Boards of Directors." *McKinsey Report Spring 2022 (3).* New York, NY: McKinsey & Company.

McNulty, E.J. and L. Marcus. June 20, 2019. "What Boards Can Do to Prepare for Crises." *Harvard Business Review.*

Menn, J and Gregg A. July 24, 2024. The Washington Post. "CrowdStrike Blames Global IT Outage on Bug in Checking Updates." Assessed on August 10, 2024. www.washingtonpost.com/business/2024/07/24/crowdstrike-microsoft-crash-bug-report/.

Ngai E., Li X and Dorothy Chau K. C. 2009. Application of data mining techniques in customer relationship management: A literature review and classification. *Expert Systems with Applications 36(2)*: 2592–2602. 10.1016/j.eswa.2008.02.021

Osterholm, M.T. and M. Olshaker. February 24, 2020. "Is It a Pandemic Yet?" *The New York Times Company.* assessed on August 10, 2024. www.nytimes.com/2020/02/24/opinion/coronavirus-pandemic.html.

Parker-Wilkins, V. 2006. "Business Impact of Executive Coaching: Demonstrating Monetary Value." *Industrial and Commercial Training* 38(3): 122–127.

Pulley, M.L. and M. Wakefield. 2001. *Building Resiliency: How to Thrive in Times of Change*. Greensboro, NC.

Ranjay Gulati, R., Nitin, N., and Franz, W. 2010. *Roaring Out of Recession*. Harvard Business Review March 2010 Edition

Snider, S. July 30, 2024. Information Week. "CrowdStrike Outage Drained $5.4 Billion From Fortune 500: Report." Accessed on August 23, 2024. www.informationweek.com/cyber-resilience/crowdstrike-outage-drained-5-4-billion-from-fortune-500-report.

Sundheim, D. 2020. *When Crisis Strikes, Lead With Humanity*, Harvard Business Review, April 23, 2020

Taleb, N.N. 2007. *The Black Swan: the Impact of the Highly Improbable*. New York, NY: Random House.

Tzu, S. 2005. *The Art of War by Sun Tzu—Special Edition*. El Paso Norte Press.

UN Climate Change. November 6, 2022a. "COP27 in Sharm el-Sheikh to Focus on Delivering on the Promises of Paris." *UN Climate Press Release*. Accessed on December 3, 2022. https://unfccc.int/news/cop27-in-sharm-el-sheikh-to-focus-on-delivering-on-the-promises-of-paris.

UN Climate Change. October 26, 2022b. "Climate Plans Remain Insufficient: More Ambitious Action Needed Now." *UN Climate Press Release*. Accessed on December 3, 2022. https://unfccc.int/news/climate-plans-remain-insufficient-more-ambitious-action-needed-now.

Wiles, J. October 21, 2022. Gartner Inc. Stamford, CT. *"What Is a Metaverse? And Should You Be Buying In?"* Accessed on November 2, 2022. www.gartner.com/en/articles/what-is-a-metaverse.

World Health Organization. February 18, 2020. "WHO Director-General's Remarks at the Media Briefing on the COVID-19 Outbreak." Assessed on 9 August 2024. www.who.int/director-general/speeches/detail/who-director-general-s-remarks-at-the-media-briefing-on-covid-19-outbreak-on-18-february-2020.

Yukl, G.A. 1989. "Managerial Leadership: A Review of Theory and Research." *Journal of Management* 15: 251–289.

About the Author

Professor Sattar Bawany is the chief executive officer of the Disruptive Leadership Institute LLC and is also concurrently the managing director and certified C-suite master executive coach with the Centre for Executive Education.

Over the past 35 years, working with global clients across various industries, Professor Bawany has delivered CEO and C-suite executive coaching engagement as well as developed a series of professional development and initiatives designed to enhance leaders' capabilities leading and engaging the workforce in the highly disruptive and digital-driven workplace.

He has assumed various senior management roles with leading global consulting firms such as Hay Group (now part of Korn Ferry), Mercer human resource consulting, Forum, and DBM (now part of Adecco).

Professor Bawany is an astute advisor to executives who need to know how they are perceived and want to focus on what is most important in their professional and personal lives. He has coached a range of leaders, from CEOs to senior vice presidents and high-potential managers. His current work in organizations focuses on encouraging individual initiative and leadership from a systemic perspective to achieve clearly defined business results. His specialty is effectively linking people processes to business outcomes.

CEO Weekly magazine in its October 2, 2023, edition, named Professor Sattar Bawany as one of the top 15 exceptional executive coaches who have had a major influence in leadership development and coaching. He was recognized as one of the "Top 10 Best CEOs in Singapore" by *CEO Insights Asia* magazine in 2023. He was also honored with the "2019 Executive of the Year for Human Resources Consulting" award during the 2019 Singapore Business Review Management Excellence Awards.

He is currently a professor of practice in disruptive leadership and an adjunct professor in business management and human resource management with various universities globally.

He holds a doctorate from the European International University Paris, an executive MBA from Golden Gate University, San Francisco, CA, and a bachelor's in business administration (marketing) from Curtin University, Perth, Western Australia.

Professor Bawany is a member of the Harvard Business Review Advisory Council. He is a fellow of the International Professional Managers Association and the Chartered Institute of Marketing. He is a professional member of the Society for Human Resource Management and the Chartered Institute of Personnel and Development. He is also a practicing member of the International Coaching Federation and the International Association of Coaching.

Index

OTHER TITLES IN THE HUMAN RESOURCE MANAGEMENT AND ORGANIZATIONAL BEHAVIOR COLLECTION

Michael J. Provitera and Michael Edmondson, Editors

- *Successful Self-Leadership* by Tim Baker
- *Nice Guys Finish Last And Other Workplace Lies,* by John Ruffa
- *Understanding and Using AI* by Daniel O. Livvarcin and Yacouba Traoré
- *The Leadership Edge* by Michael B. Ross and Mike Shaw
- *Business and Management in the Age of Intangible Capitalism* by Hamid Yeganeh
- *Ignite All* by The Fusion Team
- *(Re)Value* by Adam Wallace and Adam Wallace
- *Dysfunctional Organizations* by David D. Van Fleet
- *The Negotiation Edge* by Michael Saksa
- *Applied Leadership* by Sam Altawil
- *Forging Dynasty Businesses* by Chuck Violand
- *How the Harvard Business School Changed the Way We View Organizations* by Jay W. Lorsch
- *Managing Millennials* by Jacqueline Cripps
- *Personal Effectiveness* by Lucia Strazzeri
- *Catalyzing Transformation* by Sandra Waddock

Concise and Applied Business Books

The Collection listed above is one of 30 business subject collections that Business Expert Press has grown to make BEP a premiere publisher of print and digital books. Our concise and applied books are for…

- Professionals and Practitioners
- Faculty who adopt our books for courses
- Librarians who know that BEP's Digital Libraries are a unique way to offer students ebooks to download, not restricted with any digital rights management
- Executive Training Course Leaders
- Business Seminar Organizers

Business Expert Press books are for anyone who needs to dig deeper on business ideas, goals, and solutions to everyday problems. Whether one print book, one ebook, or buying a digital library of 110 ebooks, we remain the affordable and smart way to be business smart. For more information, please visit www.businessexpertpress.com, or contact sales@businessexpertpress.com.

www.ingramcontent.com/pod-product-compliance
Lightning Source LLC
Chambersburg PA
CBHW061316220326
41599CB00026B/4905